"Literally a 'how-to' handbook for the aspirin
to grow into the future but with appropriate attention
issues. The presentation on mission, vision, values, and leadership
will be useful for any church leader. And the discussion showing the
difference between 'borrowing money' and 'being in debt' is alone
worth the price of the book. I'm happy to recommend it."

—Eugene Habecker, President
American Bible Society

"This book will be a huge help to every pastor and board member
who faces their first church building program. Pat's solid insights will
save pastors and building committees from unnecessary and costly
mistakes that can negatively impact a church's future. Make reading
this book a requirement to be on the building committee!"

—J. David Schmidt, Leadership Consultant
J. David Schmidt and Associates

"Everyone considering building will greatly benefit from the practical and in-depth insights offered by Patrick Clements in *Proven Concepts of Church Building & Finance*. If the process is flawed, the product
will be flawed. This book will help guarantee a process that will result
in a building program free from confusion, unnecessary mistakes,
and insufficient planning."

—Alton Garrison, D.D., District Superintendent
Arkansas District Council, Assemblies of God

"For any church anticipating construction of new facilities, expansion, or relocation, Pat Clements has systematically covered every area
to lead through and accomplish a healthy, successful, and sound
project. This is the most thorough book you will read on every aspect
of building."

—Dennis A. Davis, Executive Director
Robert Schuller Ministry to Ministers

"After reading Pat Clements' new book, *Proven Concepts of Church
Building & Finance*, I thought: At last, solid, realistic, and practical
advice for all of us who need help finding our way through the
minefields of mortar and money. The book has masterfully held our
hand and walked us through one of the most difficult and confusing
leadership paths of ministry. It's a *can't miss* plan!"

—T. Ray Rachels, District Superintendent
Southern California District Council, Assemblies of God

"This is a 'must-read' book for pastors, church staff, and church leaders. It is practical and biblical, guiding us to build a congregation with a deeply spiritual mission and vision. Pat gives wise counsel for church leaders, far beyond the construction of a building."

—Jerry E. White, Ph.D., President
The Navigators

"A valuable reference guide filled with wisdom garnered from a lifetime of experience."

—B. Rupert Koblegarde, Attorney at Law

"This . . . practical and comprehensive book should be read and placed very close to church leaders' Bibles! That way it will remind them to 'count the cost' before building—and to make prayer and vision . . . a high priority for the church building process."

—John Pearson, CEO
Christian Management Association

"Every pastor who has a growing church, sooner or later is faced with a building program. *Proven Concepts of Church Building & Finance* is an excellent first step to getting you off on the right track. This book gives you a wealth of resourceful information to help develop a clear plan of action. . . . It should be part of every pastor's library."

—Dr. William Carmichael
President, Virtue Ministries
Former Publisher, Good Family Magazines

"Clements' timely insights, step-by-step process, and pragmatic realities are incredibly valuable. I don't know how anyone could start building without reading this book. A must-read for pastors, boards, congregations, and community."

—Jim Gwinn, President
Crista Ministries

"A very helpful . . . resource for pastors and congregations who are desiring to build new facilities to reach more people for Jesus Christ."

—Pastor John Palmer
First Assembly of God, Des Moines, Iowa

"I can think of no individual more highly qualified to address the subject of church financing and church building programs than my friend Pat Clements. He has had many years of experience in working with literally hundreds of churches in developing most successful programs. . . . This book will be an immense help to any and all who are contemplating enlarging programs, facilities, and influence to the glory of Christ. It contains a practical, proven methodology which can be easily adapted for practically any given situation."

—Ted W. Engstrom, President Emeritus
World Vision

"At last we have a practical readable reference book that touches on all aspects of the church building process. Patrick puts away the myth that all you need to build a church is blueprints with the passion of a pastor, the experience of a banker, and the moxie of a businessman."

—Dennis Batty, AIA
The Dennis Batty and Associates Group, Inc.
Architects and Engineers

"*Proven Concepts of Church Building & Finance* is a valuable resource . . . for any and every church, parachurch ministry, administrative office, and minister. Inspiration is on every page and is supported by workable instruction in planning, growth, building, and finance."

—Terry Raburn, District Superintendent
Peninsular Florida District Council, Assemblies of God

PROVEN CONCEPTS OF
CHURCH BUILDING & FINANCE

PROVEN CONCEPTS OF
CHURCH BUILDING & FINANCE

*A Step-by-Step Guide to
Successful Building Projects*

PATRICK L. CLEMENTS

Kregel
Academic & Professional

CONTENTS

PRAYER—A STRONG AND SECURE FOUNDATION

Only a fool would start to put up the walls of a building without first pouring a solid foundation. Yet that is precisely what we do as pastors and leaders if we initiate building plans and ministry projects without pouring a foundation of prayer. We talk a lot about prayer in the church, but in how much prayer do we actually engage?

If you're beating your head against the wall because you need to find land, you need to relocate, you need to do this or that and move forward, my challenge to you is to apply Psalm 46:10: "Cease striving and know that I am God" (NASB). No matter how packed the parking lot might be, how full the church calendar is, or how busy you are in your ministry, I believe that God is calling you to step aside into the quiet place of prayer and remember that He is still God, He is still in the heavenlies, and He hasn't forgotten about you. You are a strategic part of His plan to reach your community and the world, and you need to stop long enough to acknowledge Him, trust Him, and hear from Him.

A dear friend of mine, a fine Southern gentleman, now retired, used a line in one of his sermons that has stuck with me for the past ten or more years. He said, "When God's around, what's happening is not what's going on." So often, when we are focused on our own agenda and we're evaluating what's "going on," we're not aware of what's actually happening. Likewise, if we neglect prayer throughout the building process or gloss over it, we run the risk of missing God's miraculous purpose and plan. He has more in store for you and your congregation than just a building.

During my tenure as an associate pastor in Dublin, California, we were scouring the area looking for affordable acreage on which to build a new facility, and we had been praying seriously for God's direction for a long time. I wasn't aware at the time that He was already preparing a backslidden preacher's son to offer us a prime piece of land—and in the process to draw that man back into Christian fellowship. Even after the deal had been put together, it took me a long time to recognize that I had witnessed a phenomenal miracle in that man's life. I was so wrapped up in our having secured the wonderful property for the church that I almost missed the most significant aspect of what God had accomplished through the process. Persisting in prayer keeps us focused on what God is doing in our midst.

Start with a Season of Prayer

Prayer is so foundational to the direction and success of your ministry that I would suggest you make it your top priority. If you're not already praying consistently as leaders and as a congregation, I strongly recommend that you set aside lesser activities and initiate a time of dedicated prayer. Persist and persevere until prayer becomes a vital part of the substance of your ministry as the body of Christ. As Jim Cymbala, pastor of the Brooklyn Tabernacle, says in his book *Fresh Wind, Fresh Fire:*

> If our churches don't pray, and if people don't have an appetite for God, what does it matter how many are attending the services? How would that impress God?

Can you imagine the angels saying, "Oh, your pews! We can't believe how beautiful they are! Up here in heaven, we've been talking about them for years. Your sanctuary lighting—it's so clever. The way you have the steps coming up to the pulpit—it's wonderful. . . ."

I don't think so.

. . . What a tragedy that the quality of ministry is too often measured by numbers and building size, rather than by true spiritual results. (Jim Cymbala with Dean Merrill, *Fresh Wind, Fresh Fire* [Grand Rapids: Zondervan, 1997], 58–59.)

True spiritual results will accrue only in an atmosphere of continuous and persistent prayer. If I were you, before I took another step in the building process, I would initiate a sincere season of prayer to prepare the hearts and minds of your people to hear from the Lord what His plans are for your congregation. In addition to these times of focused prayer among your leaders and throughout the congregation, I would gather a team of committed intercessors to begin praying daily—specifically and persistently—for the church and its plans. In fact, intercessory prayer should become a strategic and central part of your building committee process.

Of course, that doesn't mean you don't act. I'm not suggesting that you pray and then sit back and expect God to drop something in your lap. Sometimes He does that, but we aren't to presume upon His methods, means, or timing. That's not what the Bible says about waiting and praying. We're told to be about the Lord's business, and that's an active phrase. Yet we can still be quiet in our spirits, still be waiting for God to open a door or to show us His direction.

When pastors are committed to prayer, when the leadership has devoted itself to prayer, and when the congregation has taken to heart the importance of prayer and has begun to fill up the prayer meetings, then your church is really ready to move forward into the vision-casting process. If you bypass prayer, your vision will all too often be weak and worldly, and that is no foundation on which to build the church of Jesus Christ. Don't try to rush through this process. Wait upon the Lord until He makes clear which direction to go. Whatever you do, don't stumble into a building project without first laying a firm foundation of prayer.

Waiting on the Lord in Prayer

I heard a great story that John Maxwell told a few years ago that illustrates beautifully the power of prayer and the wisdom of waiting on the Lord to reveal His full plan and purpose. Here's how he tells it:

> In 1981, I went to San Diego, California, and I hadn't been there very long before God began to bless and the church began to grow and people were getting saved, and I realized that we were going to run out of room real quick. . . . So I began to pray that God would give us some land.
>
> We found thirty acres not too far from our church, on the freeway, and they wanted $2 million for it. We thought for sure it would be our land. I have one hundred men in our church who pray for me every day—one hundred prayer partners. Every Sunday—I wish you could come sometime—at 7:30 you would see men walking up and down the sanctuary, laying hands on every pew, covering the sanctuary with the power of God before anybody ever comes. At eight o'clock they gather around me and lay hands on me and they pray for me and lift up my hands like Aaron and Hur. Then I go to preach and start those morning services and they all go to the Upper Room and they pray throughout the whole service in intercessory prayer for the service.
>
> I took one hundred men out to the property. I said, "Fellas, I think this will be it. I mean, look at it. It's right

on the freeway, thirty acres, just $2 million," which was not a lot of money in San Diego. I said, "Let's pray about it," and we prayed all morning.

At noon, we came back. And when we came back, we looked at each other and we all knew it wasn't the land. We walked off of that hill, and the next Sunday, I came to my people, and they thought they were going to vote on land, and I said, "We're not voting on land. It's not our property." We knew it was God, but we couldn't understand why we couldn't get that property.

The next Sunday, I preached on the subject of Elijah. Remember when, after Mount Carmel and the drought, he sent the servant out to see if there was any rain coming, and he came back and said there was a cloud the size of man's hand? That day, we passed out clouds—sticker clouds—the size of a man's hand, and we told everyone to put it on their Bibles and put it on their refrigerators and every time they saw that cloud to begin to pray for God to give us some land. And they began to pray. For three years we prayed, and all of a sudden there was some land that we wanted, but they wouldn't sell it to us because it was industrial land and open space land. We kept going back and they kept saying no. We kept saying, "But this is the property we believe God has for us."

And then, one day, they called us up on the phone and said, "Would you like to put a bid on this property?"

We said yes and we went down and they asked us what we would pay. Now they thought it was eighty acres. They weren't sure, it was not surveyed, but they thought it was eighty acres, right on the freeway in San Diego. They said, "We think it's eighty acres, give or take some. Whatever it is, that's what you get. What will you give us for it?" And we said, "We'll give you $1.8 million." And they laughed us out of the room.

I said, "Just do me a favor. Take it to the bank board."

They said they would, and the next Friday they called

and said, "We can't believe it, but we're going to sell you the land." You see, what we didn't know at that time was that they were in major trouble already in that bank, and they were trying to move property as fast as they could, and get cash as quickly as they could. And they said, "But if you're going to take it, we have to move it fast, and it's open space and you may never sell it and you may never be able to build on it," because there were so many environmental problems down there. "But," they said, "you have to take it like it is."

We said, "Fine."

And then they said, "But you have to buy water rights." And they said, "Water rights will cost you $75,000," and they gave us three times as much water rights as what we needed, and made us pay for it.

Now watch this:

They surveyed the land—and instead of eighty acres on the freeway, it was 110 acres. God just gave us thirty free acres of land in San Diego. That's as good a story as the multiplication of the loaves and fish, friends. Remember the thirty acres that we didn't buy for $2 million? He just threw it in.

The neighborhood said, "No," they didn't want us nearby. We went to a meeting and they had a petition of 227 houses. I met the guy . . . who took the petition, and I said, "Can I take you to lunch?"

He said yes, and the next day, I took him to lunch . . . and shared with him my heart and my vision. And then I looked at him and I saw that he was empty inside. I said, "Let's not talk about property; let's talk about you." And I led him to Jesus. And when I got done praying with him, he gave me a hug and said, "I'm going to go get petitions *for* you to move into our area now." The same man, five weeks later, came in with all the petitions in the neighborhood, except five, for us to move onto the property.

The planning commission said no to it; the city council said no; the county commission said no. When we got to the board of supervisors, they said yes.

Then something else happened. They were squabbling over another twenty-acre plot of ground that was between the water district and the county, and it was lipping right on our property, and there was such a squabble and it was so political and it was such a hot potato that finally they said, "We're not going to give it to either one of you, but we'll just give it to that church." And they gave us another twenty acres.

Oh, the water rights that we had to pay $75,000 for? We had a drought in San Diego. They came back two years later and said, "You know those water rights we sold you for $75,000? That was way, way, way overpriced, and you didn't need that many. Why, you only needed one-third of what we sold you."

We said, "We know that."

And they said, "Could we buy the two-thirds back that you don't want?"

We said yes, and they bought it for $150,000.

And the restrictions they'd had on the property? They'd said that we couldn't sell it to anyone else, and if we couldn't develop [the church] on that land, we'd have to give it back to the bank in five years. Now they said they would drop the restrictions, and when they dropped the restrictions, the industrialized part of the land, alone, is now [valued] between $6–8 million.

So what do we have? We have 130 acres of land on the freeway, with over a mile of frontage. And literally, when we sell off the industrial part, . . . the property will already be paid for. We will have $6–8 million in on the property; we'll have all of that land literally for free. We'll have it for free, it will all be graded, and we'll be ready to build.

Isn't God good? (John C. Maxwell, "Parenting with

Love." © 1992 John C. Maxwell. See The Injoy Group at www.injoy.com. Used by permission.)

If you earnestly pray and wait upon the Lord, will He give you 130 acres with a mile of freeway frontage? Maybe so, if that's what your church really needs. Those kinds of things do happen because we still have a miracle-working God who intervenes and accomplishes His purposes here on earth. The importance of prayer is that it helps us maintain the balance between faith (what we hope, believe, and trust God for) and reality (what we see with our own two eyes), and it keeps us focused on what God wants to accomplish *through* us, rather than on our own grand schemes.

At each stage of the building process, I encourage you to open every meeting with prayer—even when a non-Christian contractor might be attending. Keep in mind that your ultimate purpose goes far beyond mere bricks and mortar. Be diligent to bathe the entire process intentionally in prayer, and watch to see how God answers.

Seeking God's Delightful Inheritance

Psalm 16:5–6 are important verses to me: "Lord, you have assigned me my portion and my cup; you have made my lot secure. The boundary lines have fallen for me in pleasant places; surely I have a delightful inheritance" (NIV). I see these verses as a reminder that when you're walking with the Lord, He provides everything you need in proper measure. If you'll stay within the boundaries that He has ordained—whether it's the Ten Commandments, the revealed truth in God's Word, or a specific calling that He's placed on your life—there's a promise of a "delightful inheritance."

The same principles apply in the strategic planning process. If the individual members of your planning committee are praying, fasting, and sincerely seeking the mind of the Lord and His direction for the ministry of the church, the resulting vision and plans will be a reasonable depiction of God's provision for the present and His plan for your future. Once you've established the boundary lines of your vision, you will see the rich blessing of inheritance as you then earnestly pursue opportunities. And as each new "wonderful opportunity" comes along, you will have a way of evaluating them. The same is true for decisions about your building. Prayerful pursuit of your vision allows you to be deliberate and decisive as you work through the planning process, making it less likely that you will chase after the whim of the moment.

Six Focus Points for Prayer

If your church is growing and thriving, the devil is going to do everything he can to derail your efforts. Focused, ongoing, committed prayer is one means of resisting the devil and seeking the heart and mind of the Lord. As your congregation draws together to pray for the future of your ministry, focus on the following six points.

- Pray for wisdom for your pastors and other leaders.
- Pray for unity within your congregation.
- Pray for God to reveal His vision for your church.
- Pray for God's guidance in how to translate that vision into action steps that will have a positive impact in your community.
- Pray for God's timing.
- Pray for God's provision of resources to make the vision a reality.

If you will make the commitment to pray—and not move until God answers—you will be "like a man building a house, who dug deep and laid a foundation upon the rock; and when a flood arose, the river burst against that house and could not shake it, because it had been well built" (Luke 6:48 NASB). On a firm foundation of prayer, you will be ready to define your church's mission and vision.

Chapter 1

A SPECIAL NOTE TO PASTORS

BEFORE YOU RALLY YOUR congregation to start a building project, stop for a moment and assess where you are in your ministry. Are you committed to staying the course with your current congregation, or are you inclined to start looking around after a few years? If you're prone to wander, I want to challenge you to take a long-term view. Once you have established trust and built relationships within a congregation, why squander that trust by moving on to another—unknown—situation? Why not stay to reap the harvest of your years of ministry?

Over the years, I've noticed a prevailing mind-set that can settle onto pastors, especially pastors of smaller churches. It goes something like this: "I'm a pastor of a little church, so I'm kind of a little pastor. Some day I'll get a bigger church and then I'll be a bigger pastor." More often than not, it appears that "getting a bigger church" means moving somewhere else rather than building up the church where they are today. Most pastors would never come right out and make such a statement, but the attitude is reflected in the way they move from one congregation to the next. Unfortunately, "church hopping" robs both pastors of their vision for growth and longevity in their present circumstances and their congregations of stability and a long-term perspective on God's plan and provision.

Whenever I meet a pastor who expresses some variation of the "small pastor" mind-set, I'll often ask him, "How do you know that the next Billy Graham isn't in one of your Sunday school classes?"

Think about it. How big was the church that Billy Graham attended when he was a kid? I don't know if this is true or not, but the pastor of that little country church may well have thought he was fairly insignificant. But something that he modeled or taught became part of Billy Graham's spiritual foundation.

The point is not just whether you can help to raise up the next Billy Graham—because every member of your congregation is significant to God, regardless of whether they go on to become world-renowned evangelists. More importantly, the point is whether you are modeling and pouring into the lives of your people the kinds of things that will build them up and cause them to become men and women of God. Forget about how big your church is today; instead, ask yourself, "Are we growing? Do we have a vision that will lead to growth?" I've been in churches with seventy-five members who were bubbling with energy and having a tremendous impact on the surrounding community, and I've been in churches twice that size that were dead on the vine and ready to wither. The difference is vision.

My hope is that pastors will commit themselves to lives of ministry that don't include five different congregations over fifteen years, but rather one congregation with a fifteen-year track record of growth—both numerically, through evangelism, and spiritually, through discipleship. When you first consider that it takes at least seven years for a pastor to establish his ministry to the point where the congregation truly accepts his leadership and begins to trust that he isn't going to jump ship, and then that the average tenure of a pastor in the United States is close to four years, it's little wonder that many churches struggle to grow and prosper in their ministries.

Building Strong Relationships

Unless you're a young pastor fresh in the ministry or the church you're pastoring is a brand-new startup, chances are that you've been with your congregation for a while. You've built some solid relationships within the church, but you've also hemmed yourself in somewhat by the relationships you've established. Perhaps the members of your congregation have you pigeonholed as a particular type of leader, and now you're seeing the need to forge a new direction.

Whether your church is bursting at the seams or you feel a little bit stagnant, the answer is the same: You need a vision for your ministry that is born and bathed in prayer. We can all agree that everyone who's lost needs Jesus, but *how* you're going to reach them with the good news is a whole different thing. What vehicle is going to be attractive to them?

If you've been in your church for a while and you still don't have a clearly articulated mission (that goes beyond Matt. 28:19–20) and a solid, written vision statement, establishing this foundation will be a new challenge for you. You may encounter some resistance from those who think that mission and vision statements are a secular business fad that doesn't belong in the church. Some people might believe that the Great Commission is all the mission and vision that the church needs. But the truth is that a well-conceived vision undergirds every aspect of your ministry, from your sermons to your Sunday school to your plans for a new building. Without a clear mission and vision, you're sailing without charts.

The Church's Revolving Door

Why do pastors seem to feel the need to change churches on average about every four years? How much of that feeling is the result of a lack of vision and how much is based on performance? The answer will vary by individual, of course, but often a pastor will change churches out of a sense of disappointment about what he's been able to accomplish—almost an impatience that things should be moving faster or that something more should be happening. Without a vision statement in place, however, he has no accurate means of gauging progress.

After a few years, the grass starts looking greener on the other side of the fence, and the pastor starts peeking into other pastures. Invariably, his present circumstances will include some conflict with a board member or two; the pastor will have made some mistakes and might have stepped on some toes. He might be frustrated, disappointed, or discouraged because his ministry hasn't grown as rapidly as he dreamed it would or thinks it should. Depending on how a pastor manages conflict and whether he's able to deal with issues without bruising people along the way—or getting bruised himself—he may decide to persevere or choose to leave.

A variety of issues can tempt a pastor to start looking around, but they could probably be summarized as a general dissatisfaction over not accomplishing what he intended. These feelings may start with self-examination, but very often they end up focused on a particular individual or issue in the church. If you find yourself thinking, *If only that stick-in-the-mud weren't on the board, we could get something done,* or, *If we had a better building our ministry would be more effective,* you're probably already looking at greener grass in another pasture.

I've always been extremely wary of pastors who say, "If we could just get a new building, we'd be able to reach this community." My experience has been that it doesn't tend to work that way. That isn't to say that there aren't situations where a new building goes up and explosive growth follows, because that can certainly happen, but it's usually not because of the building. Perhaps a better way to approach the situation would be to say, "If we could just reach this community, then we could get the building we need." But many pastors don't look at it that way.

Writing a New Chapter in Your Ministry

God does not call a pastor to a church to fail. He may call him for a season of testing, but He doesn't call him to fail. If you're a pastor and you're disappointed with the direction of your ministry, it's time to look at the pieces of your disappointment and ask, "What can I bring to the leadership of my congregation to refocus our vision?"

What keeps you from drawing a line in the sand and saying, "OK, we've come this far. Here's where I thought we should be, but here's where we are. Using our present situation as a foundation point, what are we going to do to take our ministry to the next level?"

During my eighteen years at Church Extension Plan, we've had to refocus our vision many times. And I've had moments when I've looked over the fence at the grass on the other side, and it looked pretty green. At times, I've come into conflict with members of the board or someone on my staff. More than once, I've stepped back and asked myself, "Is God finished with me here?" If not, if I don't feel a sense of release, then what is it? Where are we supposed to be headed? To refocus vision, I usually ask myself, "If I were starting over today, where would I set the target?" That question has always energized me because it frames a problem that can be resolved.

I think that pastors too often view their tenure in a church as one long chapter, rather than the writing of a book, which includes many chapters. One of those chapters might be titled "The Period of My Discontent," but who's to say that I can't flip the page and start a new chapter without having to switch to a new book?

You are not in the middle of a long, never-ending chapter. You are in the process of writing your life's work, and if you're currently in an unpleasant chapter, recognize that there is an end to it, turn the page, and ask God to reveal what He would have you write in the next chapter. What is His vision for the next phase in your life? What is His plan for the coming season in your congregation?

Perhaps if you had a different tool or a different building, you could reach the community more effectively, but there's probably some other work that needs to be completed before you can do that. A new building is not necessarily the answer. What you need is a clear ministry vision. Once that vision is in place, it will determine the kinds of tools you need to best serve the purposes of your vision and your mission. Those tools might include new buildings, programs, or other facilities, but a building, in and of itself, will never be the answer.

Getting Unstuck and Moving Forward

Regardless of your present circumstances, recognize that God is not yet finished with the work He wants to do in your life and your ministry. He has life-long plans for you and your congregation. Stay open to the leading of the Holy Spirit and avoid becoming entrenched. At the same time, commit yourself to work toward significance rather than success.

If you are open to the ministry of the Holy Spirit in your life, then whatever you're learning—whether it's good news or bad news—will be profitable. Cultivate the attitude of a life-long student and acknowledge that you will always be learning, growing, and changing.

Regardless of your gifts, abilities, wit, and charm, it takes years to build credibility and become "the pastor" for everyone in a congregation. Most church-growth experts say that it takes seven years to really begin to accomplish a vision. If you're in a church where a series of leadership changes have occurred, it can take even longer. People can get used to the idea that the pastor isn't going to be around for very long, and they start waiting for the other shoe to drop. It's the same way in government, where career bureaucrats often wield more de facto power and influence than many elected officials simply because the bureaucrats have been there forever and will still be around after the politicians have left office. Undoubtedly, your opportunity for genuine significance in the lives of the people in your congregation will be heightened immeasurably by longevity.

If you're a new pastor or if you have been in your church for several years and have set your course, but you woke up this morning and realized that you need to jump tracks to get where you need to be; or if you haven't been operating according to a well-articulated vision and mission statement and you haven't been preparing your congregation for the next phase in the life of the church; the time to start is now.

Realistically, you should plan at least a six- to nine-month process of teaching your congregation about the church's mission and vision, biblical giving, stewardship of all areas of life, discipleship, conflict resolution, and other key issues. If this process is to become a part of the fabric of your ministry, it must be ongoing, not merely a phase that you move through and beyond.

Staying the Course

Charting a new direction may involve a very delicate training and development responsibility in the lives of your staff and other leaders. Chances are that your congregation comprises a diverse group of people who might not be prepared for the road ahead. Your task is to teach them how to become the church that God is calling them to be—without upsetting the apple cart in the process. If you're a young pastor or still new in your congregation, the job is that much tougher. But if you are genuine and sincere about staying the course and building into the lives of your people; if you're not looking at how this church is going to be a stepping stone for your next ministry call; and if you are asking God how you can pour your life into this congregation in a healthy, balanced way, then you have the opportunity to build your church into God's best vision for what it can be.

One key for staying the course is to honor the past carefully while continuing to move forward into the future. I saw this principle modeled beautifully at a church where my organization helped to finance a new building. On the same day that I was to present our program to the congregation, I had a meeting with the pastor and the board, a group of men who had grown up in the church and were now senior citizens. One of the men had been the church treasurer for thirty-five years, another had been a board member for twenty-five years, and several others had served for more than twenty years. The church itself had had only four pastors in its entire fifty-three year history. The current pastor, on the other hand, was forty-two years old and had been at the church for only four years.

Quite frankly, I thought that our proposal would encounter a lot of resistance from the board because the project involved relocating to another site and building a completely new structure. I expected the "well-seasoned" board to be resistant to change, given the fact that they had all been at the church for so long and the pastor, who was championing the cause, was relatively young and a virtual newcomer.

As I listened to the board discuss the proposal, however, I immediately began to sense the immense respect that they had for this pastor and their strong level of support for the vision that he was bringing to the congregation. The more I listened, the more I realized that the leaders were totally unified and were looking forward to the changes and the new opportunities that the new structure would open to them. I later learned that the previous pastor, who had been there for more than twenty-five years, had purchased the land and that the new pastor had been wise enough to give his predecessor tremendous honor for his foresight and leadership. The younger pastor's wisdom and discretion had certainly helped him to gain the support and approval of the board.

One essential element of long-term growth is making the decision to become a life-long learner. Commit yourself to be an active listener and a life observer. Make it part of your purpose to be a systematic reader of both Christian and secular books and magazines. If you truly desire to be an effective leader, it is essential that you continue to learn and grow.

Another key to effective leadership is creating among your leaders and laity a climate in which it's safe to fail. In fact, the only real failure comes if you fail to learn from your experiences. It's OK to preach a bad message and learn from it. It's OK to start a program, realize it isn't working, and stop it. It's OK to miss the mark, to admit that you did a lousy job, and to resolve to do it better the next time. If you take the attitude of a life-long learner, then every experience has something to teach. "And let us consider how to stimulate one another to love and good deeds . . . encouraging one another, and all the more, as you see the day drawing near" (Heb. 10:24–25 NASB).

If you can establish a learning culture in the church—one that balances excellence with mercy, redemption, and grace—then I think that your prospects are outstanding for a long-term pastoral leadership role in a healthy, supportive, and growing ministry. If, on the other hand, your own insecurities tempt you toward a bombastic style of leadership so that you often say, "I heard from God, and here's how we're going to do things," or if you create a climate in which human foibles are frowned upon and every new idea must be funneled through your own narrow perspective, chances are that eventually you're going to "hear from God" something that is going to fall flat on its face. What happens then? Did God fail?

I get very concerned when I hear pastors talking about what I would call "revelation management," which can be summed up in the statement, "God told me . . . therefore, get on board." I have no problem with the idea that God gives pastors guidance, but I get nervous when the only way that a congregation can determine its direction is for the key leader to say, "Well, God told me this." It's far better to have a process by which the goals, plans, and objectives of the ministry are defined and developed by all of the stakeholders in the organization who are individually and collectively seeking the mind and will of the Lord. Consensus building is not a foreign concept in the church of Jesus Christ.

Bringing Your Vision to the Board

As you continue to learn and discover new things, it's never too late to start establishing the right kind of leadership principles. As the result of new insight or conviction, you might experience seasons in leadership during which you will have to stop what you're doing and say, "Whoa, I need to repent of this attitude, or that process, or this communication style." Begin to foster a climate of openness. Make allowances for human error, but learn from your mistakes and endeavor not to repeat them. Pursue a more collaborative style with your board or leadership team. I believe it's perfectly appropriate for a pastor to sit down with the church board and say, "I've been doing a lot of thinking and praying and reading about leadership and I recognize that I've been too domineering. Based on this new understanding, I want to change my leadership style and draw you guys into a more collaborative effort—but I need your help to do that."

Far too often we try to hide our insecurities and shortcomings from others, rather than confessing our faults and learning to shore up each other's weaknesses. How refreshing it is when a pastor or other leader can admit that he doesn't have it all figured out. Everybody already knows it, but when somebody brings it out into the open in a spirit of humility, it frees everyone to be more honest and vulnerable. A climate of openness also liberates creativity and vision, which is exactly what your congregation wants and needs from its leaders.

Answer the following questions as honestly as you can, and resolve to take any necessary action to get your ministry, leadership, and congregation back on course.

1. Do I need to mend bridges or correct some misunderstandings with members of the church board or planning committee?

2. Do we have a clear focus on where we're going?
3. Are we unified in that focus?
4. How extensively have we communicated our mission and vision to the congregation?
5. How many people genuinely share the vision? Is it just the key leaders?
6. What are the chances that we'll successfully accomplish the goals of our vision?
7. Have we assessed our ability to move forward?
8. Am I certain that the proposed changes—the new building or whatever it is—are for the benefit of the ministry and the congregation and not just because I want to erect a monument?

If you've answered these questions sincerely and honestly, you probably have a pretty good focus on what needs to be done to set the stage for a successful committee process.

Disaster Recovery Plan

It's never too late to start doing the right thing. If your congregation has launched into a building project without first establishing its mission and vision, stop the process now and get everyone on the same page. If you have an agreed-upon vision and you've strayed from it, you would be well advised to put on the brakes and say, "I think we're headed down a course for calamity. Let's pause and take another pass at this." It's better to stop and reconsider than to push forward and create a real disaster—even if you have already spent a lot of money in the process. Don't throw good money after bad. Even if you feel that your credibility as a leader is at stake, it is far better to take a step back, reevaluate the situation, acknowledge any errors that have been made, deal with whatever fallout has resulted from those errors, and then reconnect to a more focused vision and direction.

If you don't make a course correction now, more and more

people will eventually begin to realize that your project is going in the wrong direction, and criticism will grow until a breakdown finally occurs somewhere. As grim as it might seem to change course, you are far wiser to regroup now and say, "Let's not walk off this cliff we are headed toward. What have we learned together in this process? Let's use this new information to get our project on the right track."

As difficult as it is to step forward and admit mistakes, especially if you're primarily responsible for the road you're on, it's an opportunity to model humble leadership to the body and bring everyone along to a new sense of purpose, focus, and consensus. Swallow your pride and say, "Hey, friends, we have some new information that suggests we're headed for disaster. I realize that I've led us this far, and I accept responsibility for my part, but for the long-term good of this church, we need to make a course correction."

Of course, you will always have folks who say, "I told you so," but even those situations can be turned to good if you can avoid becoming defensive. Rather than trying to justify yourself, simply say, "You know, brother, you were more right than I realized. I appreciate that you rang the warning bell, and I'm sorry that we didn't listen to it sooner. Now, can you help us reconnect to a focused vision? Let's get this going on the right path."

There will also be those who say, "Wait a minute, there's nothing wrong with the direction we're going." To those people you have to say, "Let's look together at this new information and let's talk this through." Take the time to explain the need for clarifying the church's mission and vision so that everyone can pull back into alignment and remain supportive.

My experience with projects that have started in the wrong direction, and where no corrective action was taken, has been that, ultimately, more and more people jump off the bandwagon until the pastor is the only one riding it over the cliff.

When course corrections become necessary, your vision statement will be critical for establishing a renewed consensus. When you find yourself going down a wrong road and need to back up, it's time to reevaluate your vision. If your vision was carefully crafted based on your mission statement, it's more likely that you've strayed from your vision than that the vision itself is wrong. Either way, lessons can be learned in the process. Remember, the life of the church is an unfolding story, and part of that story is learning how to work together to overcome mistakes and make the most of your opportunities. Now is the time to pull together as the body of Christ and forge a new direction that will take you toward your desired outcome.

Chapter 2

VISION: DON'T BREAK GROUND WITHOUT IT

THE FIRST STEP IN THE church-building process—before you start talking about remodeling your building, adding on, or moving to a new site—is to sit down and define your church's mission and vision. So much has been written in the past fifteen years about defining one's corporate and personal mission and vision that the idea of writing mission and vision statements is almost a cliché. Unfortunately, after the dust has settled, far too many businesses—and churches—still operate without a definitive mission and vision.

If you don't have a clearly articulated mission statement, or if you haven't developed your vision to the extent that you can reasonably project where your congregation is headed over the next five to ten years, you really have no business thinking about a building project. You need to clarify your mission and your vision first.

Our Mission: Why We Exist

The mission of the church declares God's *specific* purpose for planting your local congregation in your community. Simply stated, your mission statement expresses why you exist as a congregation. It's not enough to adopt Matthew 28:19–20 or Mark 16:15 as the mission for your church. As spiritual as it may sound to say "make disciples of all the nations," the question remains how you are going to translate this global mandate to the local level. You must develop a specific, God-ordained mission statement for *your* church in *your* community so that you can focus on accomplishing God's specific call for *your* body of believers.

One mission statement that I particularly like is the following from a church in Washington state:

> Our Mission is to honor and follow the Lord Jesus through:
>
> 1. Gathering believers in both congregational and small group settings to unite in dynamic praise and worship and to share in authentic New Testament relationships.
> 2. Reaching the lost and the unchurched, first in our city and surrounding area, and also around the world.
> 3. Discipling the found and equipping those who come to Him that they might walk in the Lordship of Jesus Christ, the light of God's Word, and the fullness of the Holy Spirit.
> 4. Meeting the needs of a hurting world by employing relevant, creative, practical, and spiritual means to demonstrate the compassion and healing power of Christ.

A mission statement can also be a simple statement that captures the essence of your congregation's purpose, as do the following examples:

- To know Jesus Christ and to make Him known.
- To exalt Jesus Christ, become His fully devoted followers, and share His grace and truth with all people.

The most important aspect of your mission statement is that

it becomes a rallying point, a unifying principle, for defining the vision of the church.

Our Vision: Where We Are Headed as a Congregation

Out of your mission statement will grow a vision statement that will express specifically *how* you intend to accomplish the mission of the church. The *mission* statement is what you get up every morning and do. The *vision* statement expresses where you expect to be at checkpoints A, B, C, and D as you work toward accomplishing your mission. According to Christian management consultant J. David Schmidt, an effective vision statement will be:

- Aligned with God's will as you understand it: Where do you see God working?
- Challenging: A compelling vision moves people to great things. What would personally challenge you?
- Stated visually: It paints a word picture.
- Stretching: It will take the congregation and leadership beyond typical thinking and action patterns.
- Achievable: Although stretching, a well-conceived vision is seen as possible.
- Emotional: Generates enthusiasm and a desire for change. Touches the heart as well as the mind.
- Clear: Can be understood—even by organizational outsiders.
- Focused: Directs the energy of your congregation toward one clear outcome.
- Future oriented: A vision is forward looking, not a statement about the present.
- Short and snappy: One to two pages, written in an upbeat style.
  (Adapted from a "Vision" worksheet developed by J. David Schmidt and Associates, © 1997. Used by permission.)

To what J. David Schmidt said, I would add the following essential components of a well-cast vision:

- Aligned with the mission: Your vision statement should be a clear enunciation of how you believe your ministry will look if you faithfully pursue your mission.
- Grounded in reality: Based on your internal and external strengths, weaknesses, opportunities, and threats (SWOT analyses—discussed in greater detail later) and your demographic study of the community, your vision statement should address real issues and real concerns in your congregation, neighborhood, and city.
- Balanced with your budget: Big dreams are easy to formulate, but, based on your priorities, what can you afford? Ask God to expand your capabilities.

Your vision statement should include information about each key area of ministry in your church, including worship, preaching, music, youth, outreach, fellowship, administration, prayer, missions, service, Christian education for adults and children, etc.

A well-written vision statement will give focus, dimension, and purpose to your ministry plans. Only after the vision statement is in place can you determine what sort of buildings and other facilities you really need. If your vision is to be a family-oriented church, for example, your building will naturally include adequate classrooms and nursery space to meet the needs of growing families. If, on the other hand, you see your congregation as an evangelistic point of celebration in the community, a large sanctuary and foyer would be essential, and classroom space might be secondary. If your vision includes feeding the homeless and hungry in your community, you'll need to design a building in a strategic location and with sufficient access, food-service capability, storage, and serving space. In short, your vision defines the type of facility you need.

Designing an appropriate church building depends as much

on your ability to figure out who you are as a congregation as it does on architecture, construction, and financing. The design should support the congregation's cohesive and compelling vision of the future around which every member can rally and toward which they can work. A carefully crafted vision statement will help you devise a logical plan of attack. Without a clear purpose and a definition of priorities, you will likely delay, if not derail, your prospects for expansion.

Start by selecting a planning team of five to seven individuals who will consult with key stakeholders in the church to gather input for developing a vision statement. A well-conceived mission and vision statement should tap into the passionate heart of the church and create excitement, energy, and motivation to see the mission accomplished. If it doesn't, then you've probably missed the mark.

In his book *The Monk and the Riddle,* author Randy Komisar draws a distinction between *passion* and *drive.* Passion, he says, *"pulls* you toward something you cannot resist" whereas drive *"pushes* you toward something you feel compelled or obligated to do." If your vision statement says more about your *drive* than your *passion,* maybe you should take another crack at it. It's worth the additional effort because your vision statement will be the guiding influence in all of your decisions about ministry, building, and growth.

Why Is Vision Important?

A vision statement is like a road map; it gives you a track on which to run. In any given situation, I could probably make a case for constructing twenty different styles of buildings and a *compelling* case for maybe half of those ideas. But which is the right one for your particular church? The answer depends completely on where you see your congregation downstream. What is your mission? Why do you exist as a congregation in your specific location at this time? How do you see your ministry developing over the next five or ten years? Either you put vision first, or you end up grasping at thin air when the time comes to make decisions about your building. Doing the necessary work at the vision level answers so many questions down the road or at least gives you a good framework for making decisions. It really is a vital step.

A clear vision brings other decisions into focus. For example, I'm familiar with a family-oriented congregation in California that recently acquired a building designed as a worship center. It has everything you want in an auditorium—a full balcony, excellent acoustics, good sight lines, and seating for nine hundred. The one major drawback is that the building has maybe four classrooms in it, enough to serve only fifty to one hundred people. The facility has an adequate nursery and toddler area and a small chapel but virtually no adult classrooms.

At first glance, in light of the strong family basis of the congregation, one might assume that the church leaders made a questionable decision in purchasing this building. Clearly, they will either have to add classroom space or build a separate classroom building (probably within the next three years), to meet the needs of the congregation. On the other hand, the building they purchased represents a wonderful opportunity because in addition to the nice sanctuary, the property has ample parking to support the church's growth whereas their previous building had very limited parking. The point here is that their vision statement allowed them to weigh the various factors underlying their decision to move and made it possible for the pastor and the board to lead the church forward into a reasonable purchase and relocation. Also, based on their vision statement, the next strategic step is very clear: they must increase their classroom space.

Visionary Leadership

Any discussion of the mission or vision of the church necessarily begins with the pastor because God has placed the pastor in a position to shepherd and lead the flock. This doesn't mean that he does all of the work himself or that the vision is all his, but rather that he must take the initiative to get the leadership board and the congregation on the right track.

When most pastors are preparing to enter the ministry, they have at least some idea of what they would like to accomplish. However, unless they've had the privilege of being reared in a church that is well structured, their vision is usually fairly immature because they are inexperienced. All too often, they see themselves preaching to throngs of people, but they don't really think about the implications of that kind of ministry on the infrastructure of the church. What kind of facilities do they need to accommodate all of those people? And what other services and ministries does the church need to offer outside of Sunday morning worship? Young pastors often think in terms of only the sanctuary and not what's going on in the rest of the building.

After a pastor has gained experience with a couple of growing congregations—perhaps he started in a smaller church and then moved along in his ministry to a larger congregation, or maybe he has lived and grown with a single congregation long enough to have made his initial mistakes and learned how to recover from them—he begins to get a more well-rounded concept of what it takes to minister effectively to a growing congregation. For example, he understands that you can't house the junior high group in the same kind of room where you put the third graders. The youth group needs its own space where they can have skateboarding posters and foosball tables. The high school and college groups may have entirely different needs. And he has learned the kinds of questions to ask when evaluating the future facility needs of the church.

If the body life of the church includes family gatherings and church socials, is a sizable fellowship hall available to accommodate them? What is the church's outreach into the community, and how do those activities affect the building? All of these issues—how best to accommodate the dynamic needs of a congregation—are vital for effective growth. The specific segments of the church where ministry will be focused all grow out of the mission of the church.

I've seen very successful ministries that each have a very large sanctuary and a few rooms for taking care of small children, but everything else is done in cell groups or small gatherings outside the church walls. Even Sunday school sometimes takes place in homes or a nearby school. It's not a model to which I would subscribe personally, but it's one that has worked. The bottom line is that each congregation has to identify what kind of body it wants to be and which direction they're heading because those issues have a great deal to do with how far out they have to think in terms of their building and how rapidly they have to make the change. It's important that the pastor be on top of these issues and ready to lead the congregation through the planning and decision-making process.

Building on Your Strengths

A key part of translating the mission of the church (why we exist) into a compelling vision (how we intend to live out our mission) is to meet with your key leaders to evaluate the current strengths and weaknesses of your congregation and to identify the opportunities and threats that you face. This exercise—which focuses attention on your strengths, weaknesses, opportunities, and threats—is called a SWOT analysis, and the format can be as simple as four columns on a sheet of paper. What's important is that you take the time to explore thoroughly each of the four categories as it relates to your congregation and the mission and vision of your church.

Defining Your Community

Next, you should do a demographic study of your congregation and the community that you are trying to reach to begin focusing your vision on the unique needs and opportunities in your area. It is often easiest to start with your local chamber of

Strengths	Weaknesses	Opportunities	Threats

commerce and public library to get data on your ministry area. In addition, you often can get data from your city hall and county offices. The Internet is a growing source of information that should be explored. Don't assume that you know what everyone needs without testing it. If you don't get out there and ask the questions, you can miss your goal by an absolute mile. No doubt we've all heard of a ministry somewhere that failed to recognize the changing demographics of its community and ended up either limping along ineffectively or closing its doors altogether. Tapping into the changing profile of your community is essential if you want to successfully meet people's long-term needs.

What is the demographic composition of your community? Is it a suburban bedroom community, full of commuters and busy families who are into fast food, convenience, consumerism, and quality, or is it an inner-city community with a lot of single-parent homes, ethnic diversity, poverty, and other social issues? All of these factors will influence your ministry decisions. If you are an urban, inner-city church, more likely than not your ministry will be cross-cultural, with opportunities for recreational activities and service to young people and maybe people in crisis. Even if you define yourself as a family church, social realities exist in many communities that you had better take into consideration if you want to reach people. Are there a lot of single parents or double-income households in your area? Perhaps your ministry will take shape around after-school care. Your outreach might include boys' and girls' clubs and sports programs, spiritual formation classes, and youth activity groups. If the public schools are not good, or a strong demand exists for good private schools, you might be able to serve your community best by organizing and operating a school.

The depth and scope of your demographic study will vary according to the size of your community. If your church is in a large city, you may get valuable information from the chamber of commerce or local civic organizations. In a small town, your study might consist of having coffee in all of the local hangouts and getting to know the movers and shakers in your town.

A demographic study and a needs analysis in your community will suggest certain directions for your ministry. The trick is to match the gifts in your congregation with the needs in the community. If you have a church full of people with a particular set of gifts, abilities, and interests, then you'll want to find an expression of ministry for those gifts that meet the needs in your community. Otherwise, people become frustrated and either try to do things for which they're not gifted or leave the church to go someplace where they can express their gifts. If you notice certain groups of people in your church who are particularly gifted or have a passion in a certain area, it makes sense to try to link them with a ministry. To the extent that their ministry creates needs within your existing building, you have one more factor to consider in your planning process. It makes good sense to build around your strengths, gifts, and passions in relation to the needs in your community. If you find that there's a need but you don't have the gifts or the interest within your congregation to meet it, try to network with other ministries that can provide what is needed.

I know of several urban churches that would do well to have a good sports program, but they don't have the affinity or the equipment to do it. Unless your church is large enough to bring someone on staff who has the necessary qualifications, it's better to stay away from areas of ministry that you aren't equipped to do. You don't want to show up for basketball dressed in gym shorts, black socks, and wing tips and ruin your credibility. On the other hand, don't shy away from meeting the needs in your community just because you feel inadequate. God has a way of working through our weaknesses.

Once you get into the demographic and needs-assessment process, a lot of these things become evident. But it depends on paying attention to what is going on around you. Regardless of the size of your community, there is no substitute for getting into the neighborhood to meet people and discover their causes and concerns firsthand. You really need to go to the coffee shops, the supermarkets, the town hall meetings, and listen to what's going on. The best way to evaluate the needs in your community is to get to know the people.

Based on the information from your demographic study, you can further refine your SWOT analysis as those key factors become evident within the context of the needs in your community. As you compare these results with your emerging vision statement, list and review the strengths and weaknesses of your current facility and develop a list of needs, wants, and dreams for upgrading, expanding, or replacing your building.

- *Needs.* Features and accessories that you *must have* in your building to meet the minimum requirements of your current ministry and future vision. For example, you might determine that you need a sanctuary that seats at least 250 and nursery or child-care facilities that will accommodate 25 babies and toddlers.
- *Wants.* Features that would be nice to have to enhance your ministry but that are not essential. Items in this category might include recreational space for youth programs and a flexible wall design in the sanctuary to allow for overflow seating.
- *Dreams.* Things that would be delightful to have if the

opportunity presented itself to enrich your current ministry and allow for your anticipated growth. Dreams will vary from one congregation to the next, but they might include such things as a sports facility, a counseling center, or a Christian school.

If you have a congregation of one hundred people in a small town and your demographic study reveals that fifty percent of the population is made up of two-paycheck families who commute to a nearby town to work, and there's a need for child care, athletic activities, and relationship building, then maybe your long-term vision will include a day-care center, a sports ministry program, and a counseling ministry. Maybe you can launch your athletic program by using the local high school facilities one night a week, but as you grow and gain financial footing as a congregation, your vision would be to build a gymnasium with fellowship space and classrooms.

At the outset, you want to define how your organization will look, what kinds of ministry you will offer to the community, and what type of facilities you will need to house those ministries. Maybe your best-case scenario suggests that five years down the road your congregation will have grown to five hundred members, but you still won't be able to afford a gymnasium. If you believe that the sports program is really an effective piece of your ministry, perhaps you should secure a long-term deal with the high school to use their facilities and use your available dollars to expand your present classroom space into a first-rate day-care facility with dual-use capabilities for Sunday mornings.

It is equally true for a church of fifty members or five thousand members that they need a clear understanding of their five-year vision to determine what they need to build. The scope and scale may vary, but the underlying principles are absolutely the same. Regardless of the size of your church or town, all of the principles that we have discussed apply. You may customize your vision and plans to fit your situation, but don't think that you're too small or too big to stay within the boundaries. Remember, God is interested in every corner of the world, including your community. If you've been called as a pastor or leader in your church, you're there for a reason. Make the most of it for God's glory.

Values: Our Central Guiding Principles

In addition to your mission and vision, it is important to articulate your values clearly. Values are the guiding principles or boundary lines that you will not move or go beyond. For example, at Church Extension Plan we have identified the following unifying principles to guide our business.

- We will serve God based on His Word and follow the leading of the Holy Spirit with our ministry.
- We will commit ourselves to the pursuit of excellence and professionalism.
- We will seek opportunities to serve.
- We will manage with goals and objectives.
- We will respond to all clients individually and with high esteem.
- We will strive for high-quality and personal customer service.
- We will function with integrity.
- We will know God corporately, keep Him central, and exercise every opportunity to serve Him and make Him known to others.
- We are committed to the concept that individuals shall be treated honorably, encouraged, rewarded, informed, and properly assigned work, giving meaning to their efforts and challenging their minds.
- We are committed to excellence in communication, both internally and externally.
- We will model and communicate biblical principles of stewardship.

Based on your mission, vision, and values, you will want to develop a ministry plan that defines the strategies and action steps for accomplishing your mission and vision. A ministry plan is not complete until it includes specific action steps with timelines for the completion of each step, which will ensure that the agenda is moving forward.

It is essential to an effective plan that you persevere until you have a means of measurement and a timeline for all action steps, breaking every strategy into detailed steps that will advance you toward your objective. Ask yourself, "What must happen first to move this project forward?" Then, "What is the next step?" Continue the process until every step is defined and you are able to see how the project will be completed. These ideas did not originate with me—in fact, they might be called Planning 101—but they are very basic and essential to accomplishing your objectives as a congregation.

Once you have identified your mission and clarified your values, they should remain fairly static. "Why you exist" should not be subject to change, and the principles by which you live shouldn't waver. Your vision will remain somewhat stable, but it is open to periodic review and revision. Strategies will change and adapt according to circumstances in your community, and your action steps will be even more fluid. Overall, the system should be flexible. You won't be changing your mission every few years, but you may be fine-tuning your vision as you begin to express it and start to see that, "Whoa, we really missed it here. We should have pursued that opportunity more vigorously. We could do much better." Or, "We were way overblown in our expectations; we need to pull in the sails."

Collaboration and Communication

The vision-casting process does not take place in a vacuum or a cloister in which a select committee sits staring at a blank wall trying to dream up a vision that will meet the needs of the outside world. Likewise, a good mission and vision statement is not the work of one person. It should be the collaborative handi-work of a group of people who have a shared burden and are really working together.

As you seek to define your church's vision, the goal is to combine *clarity* with *commonality,* as opposed to vagueness and diversity. If your vision is clear but with diverse points of view, the result will be fragmentation. Even worse, if the vision is vague and with diverse points of view, the result will be disinte-gration. A vague vision with common points of view creates frustration because people have a lot of commonality, but they don't know where they're going. But a clear vision with com-mon points of view creates cohesion because it gets everyone moving in the same direction.

VISION IN FOCUS

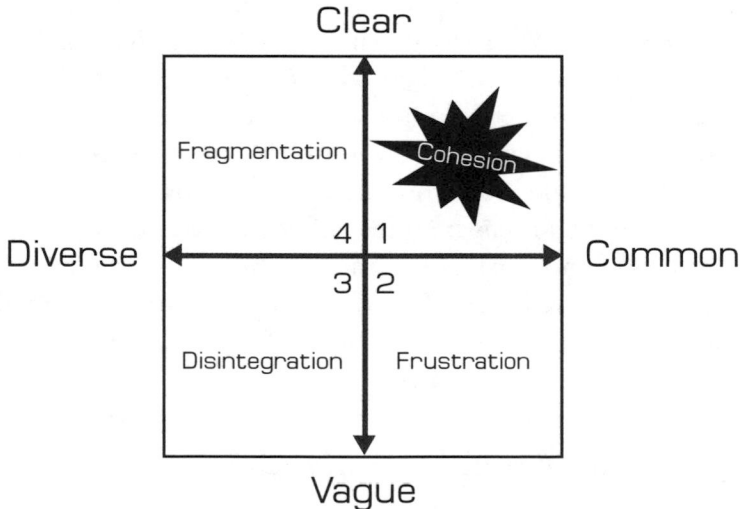

According to J. David Schmidt, "a clear and common vision builds cohesion and thwarts fragmentation, disintegration, and frustration within your ministry" and "acts as glue to bind a work team together and to focus efforts on the agreed-upon right things. This [Vision in Focus] chart shows how vision in an organization can be all over the place. Only when a work team's vision is clear *and* common (in quadrant #1) can there be cohesiveness" (italics mine).

How to Write a Vision Statement

The vision statement is a picture of how you think the future will look at certain mileposts if you achieve your mission, a series of snapshots of how you see your church at various points down the road. To help you get started with the vision-casting process, we've adapted the following questions from J. David Schmidt and Associates.

"As you ask the Lord for His thoughts and direction on this effort, there are two passages you may want to read and reflect on which demonstrate the role vision plays in effective leadership, and the power God has to open your eyes: Nehemiah 2 and Mark 8."

Questions to ask yourself. (Not all of these need to be answered, but use them to prompt your thinking.) Use future-oriented and activity-related words to communicate your vision effectively.

1. If God answered one prayer about the *preferred* future of the ministry of your church, what would that prayer and its answer be?
2. When you close your eyes and dream about the future of your congregation, what do you see?
3. What is the biggest difference you see between this past year of ministry and your vision of what it will be two years from now? What other significant differences do you foresee?

4. What will be the primary thrust or focus of ministry five years from now?
5. Where will this ministry be occurring?
6. What will your congregation be striving for and measuring?
7. What will you not be doing that you are doing now?
8. What distractions will no longer be present?
9. What size will your congregation be?
10. How will you accommodate any additional growth? (Adapted from a "Vision" worksheet developed by J. David Schmidt and Associates, © 1997. Used by permission.)

Now that you have your vision in front of you, do you feel a sense of urgency or just kind of flat? Your vision should be visual, but it also must be visceral. The reading of the vision statement ought to stir people (in a good way) and create enthusiasm—a sense of "Wow! If we're going to do all that, we had better get moving." Your vision statement should bring cohesion to your congregation, like a magnetic force that pulls everyone toward the goal. If reading the vision statement doesn't ignite some positive energy, some passion, and some enthusiasm throughout the congregation, then you haven't hit the bull's-eye.

Usually, if your vision statement is compelling, challenging, and stretching, you'll look at it and say, "We're not all of that. Still, it's something for which we're striving, reaching, and praying." Stretching to reach your vision will include asking some of your current members to acquire new skills or finding additional people who already have the skills, gifts, and passions you need.

A Timeline for Developing Your Vision Statement

Laying the groundwork for an effective vision is an ongoing exercise. Ideally, with a series of meetings, the vision-casting process should take no longer than one month, and your mission and vision statements should be in place several months before you start the building process. It's never too late to start defining your vision, but it's also never too early. Developing, implementing, and revising the vision statement should be a regular, ongoing part of the life of the church. But if you're starting from scratch, it will probably take between six and nine months to get the congregation up to speed without their feeling manipulated or like you're lowering the hammer on them. You don't want your congregation to get the impression that you're suddenly saying, "Here's what *we're* going to do, and *you're* going to pay for it."

After you have defined the vision, the rest of the process is a matter of timing. Where are you in terms of your stewardship life compared to what you're trying to accomplish? How extensive or complex a project will be necessary to achieve your objectives? It's never too early to do some general planning, but if some key elements are not yet in place, it's probably too early to get specific—nuts and bolts and hard lines—because things will change as you gain experience with your plan.

The planning process is an ongoing continuum of planning, working, and learning, because as you do the work you learn new things that affect the plan and move it forward. Similarly, with the emergence of a vision, undoubtedly the vision is going to change shape over five years. Somewhere in the process, your vision will take on different dimensions, which may affect how the ultimate building will look. So you don't want mechanical drawings done too early in the process.

A clear, common, and cohesive vision will help you determine whether you need to upgrade, remodel, add to, or replace your church facility somewhere along the way. From your vision, then, will grow not only a set of goals and strategies but also action steps for accomplishing your goals.

Chapter 3

VISION SHARING

THE WIDER YOU CAST your net for input during the vision-development process, the more involved your congregation will be and the more representative the resulting vision will be. The size of the group depends on the size of your church, but at a minimum you should include all staff members (associate pastors, youth pastor, music pastor, etc.), elders or deacons, key volunteers, and other stakeholders. You would certainly want to solicit input from anyone in the congregation who is already excited about the ministry of the church or who is passionate about a particular area of service.

Who Else Should Be Involved in the Vision-Casting Process?

Even a small church with only one pastor and a small board has other key people who should be involved in the vision-casting process, including those who faithfully support the ministry of the church and those who are there every Sunday to open the doors and turn on the lights. Some of these individuals might not be visionary thinkers, but that's OK. You still want them involved because they are committed to the mission and ministry of the church. They might not be able to think in a visionary way, but they probably have a pretty good handle on the current state of the congregation. So, for example, if you say, "I think we seem pretty friendly and outgoing as a body," they might be able to say, "I don't think that's true. I think we're pretty tightly knit and not terribly open to newcomers." It is simply essential to pull together open-minded folks who are willing to look dispassionately at the reality of the situation facing your church. Don't be afraid. What's important is to draw in diverse points of view to begin working toward a common perspective.

The only person you don't want on the committee is the guy who automatically says that any way that's different is wrong. At some point, you will have to address the naysayer's concerns, but not necessarily at the meeting where you're trying to cast the vision because he'll torpedo everything that comes up. If possible, keep the curmudgeons on the sidelines until you're through with the vision-casting process.

If, despite your best efforts, you end up with a stick-in-the-mud on your committee, here's how you can work with him and keep your process moving forward.

1. Make your initial meeting a "brainstorming" session. In a true brainstorming process, everyone at the table tosses in their ideas without comment or criticism. Every positive idea has equal weight and is encouraged and written down. No negative topics are allowed, and no ideas are criticized or debated. The purpose of brainstorming is to encourage creative thinking and get every possible idea out on the table, no matter how far-fetched it might sound at first. For this to work, you must explain the rules of brainstorming beforehand and enforce them consistently during the session.

2. The second phase of this strategy is an evaluation meeting in which every idea from the brainstorming session is reviewed to determine what's realistic and what's not. Some ideas might be too ambitious for the size of your church,

whereas others might require further research before their feasibility can be ascertained. Don't be too quick to discard an idea, though. Sometimes a suggestion that sounds nutty or too formidable during the brainstorming session starts to make sense when you take a closer look.

This two-step brainstorming and evaluation process can be extremely useful even if you don't have a stubborn mule on your committee. The main purpose of brainstorming is to free people's creativity and get the ideas flowing. At the very least, it gets the process started without barriers, and you might be surprised at some of the great ideas that emerge in a no-holds-barred brainstorming session. By modeling an open and receptive attitude as a leader, you can facilitate the proceedings, helping people overcome their shyness or fear that their ideas will be ridiculed or disregarded. And by following your brainstorming session with a separate meeting to evaluate each idea critically, the concerns of the "no change" or "slow change" folks can be addressed in due time.

Opinion Leaders and Fringe Players

When selecting your vision-casting committee, it's important not to be too exclusive. You don't want only people who agree with you, and you certainly don't want to limit your group to people who think that you're the greatest pastor who ever walked the earth. Identify key opinion leaders early in the process and be sure to include them, especially if they are nonvisionaries. Involving them early allows them to see the vision unfold and gives them a stake in the outcome—as long as you don't allow their lack of vision to hamper the progress of the committee. But be prepared; your skills as a facilitator will most certainly be tested.

Vision-casting is a great opportunity to enfold the "silent savants" from your congregation—those people who you know have great ideas but never say anything—into the life of the church. You want to include some people who are a little bit "edgy" but who are still stakeholders, because it allows you to avoid what might otherwise become a blind spot, and it gives you an opportunity to test the emerging vision with some folks who might be skeptical. If you can draw in the edgy ones and get them to buy in to the vision right from the start, then you know that your vision statement is compelling.

A church is like a target—a series of concentric rings. The first couple of rings at the center of the target comprise your core group. The objective of ministry is to draw people in who are out on the edges and keep them moving closer and closer to the center. A good indicator of a well-crafted vision is that it attracts people who are out on the fringe of your ministry as well as those at the core. That's what you want.

I cannot overstate the importance of making the vision-casting process collaborative. One of the most dangerous situations for a pastor is when he articulates a unilateral vision and the congregation murmurs its assent out of respect for the pastor's role, but they never truly embrace the vision. A lot of pastors confuse "assent" with "commitment," only to be caught off-guard when it's time to vote, make a faith promise pledge, or maybe even write the check. Suddenly, the tide of opinion changes, and it doesn't go the way the pastor anticipated. Instead of climbing aboard the bandwagon, the congregation says, "Time out, Pastor. This was really *your* idea."

There's a big difference between casual assent and full-hearted commitment. Far too often, church leaders focus on "getting pledges" rather than building a sense of participation and ownership in the vision. The more people you include in the vision-casting process, the greater your chances of building a committed core of active members who will pray and work and contribute to make the vision a reality.

Building Consensus

As the process moves forward, it's important that you communicate effectively with your congregation. If you're wise, you will involve as many people as you reasonably can in the early planning stages and immediately begin to build consensus. Congregations of growing and vital churches usually have a vibrant core of committed individuals who can become effectively involved in the new project. These important players, who often are opinion leaders in the church, can be instrumental in building enthusiasm and support throughout the congregation.

It is almost impossible to over-communicate during the vision-casting and early planning stages of your building design. Remember, the members of your congregation will not only be using the facility but also be asked to pay for it. If your members feel that they are involved from the beginning, they will be more likely to support the plans financially when the time comes. But don't wait. The process of fundraising should begin as soon as you have consensus that it is time to begin a building project.

Depending on the culture of the community and the composition of your congregation, relocation can present some unique challenges for communication and buy-in. A physical relocation of an existing congregation is always unsettling, unless the congregation has been renting and the move will mean finally having a home of your own. In the case of churches that have been renting facilities, the prospect of permanence and putting down some roots usually gets everybody excited and willing to make the move. Of course, some people will always get upset no matter what you do, so don't be discouraged.

If a move is going to be required, don't overlook the emotional ties that members of the congregation have with your current building—even if it's an old place with poor lighting and no air conditioning. When people can say, "I was baptized in this building" or "I was saved right over there," it is going to be difficult to move. In the course of life, people go through incredible times of joy, grief, soul searching, and worship inside a church building, and they naturally identify their significant memories with the location. Hearing the pastor or the chairman of the elder or deacon board say, "We're selling our building to a bowling alley" (or even, "We're selling our building to another congregation") often doesn't set well with members of the body who have an emotional investment in the current facility.

We must help our congregation realize that the church is not the building but rather the people, but at the same time we can't lose sight of or minimize the fact that many people have strong emotional ties to the building. The key is to paint a vivid picture of the purpose and vision for the new facility. Effective communication with your congregation can alleviate many potential problems surrounding a move. And if the vision is widely shared and supported, it gives a rationale, a framework, for moving the ministry of the church to a more suitable facility.

A congregation's perspective of "what is the church?" can have either a limiting effect or an invigorating effect on the vision of the church. World War III could result if conflict arises over a narrowly supported vision that dictates a move from the existing building. Of course, in some congregations a civil war would ensue if you suggested something as simple as replacing the old pews with stacking chairs for more flexibility.

Communicating the Vision to the Congregation

As the most visible leader in the church, the pastor must be the primary communicator of the vision through a combination of approaches, including special meetings, little vignettes on Sunday morning, and written communication. Be sure to communicate in a variety of ways—orally, visually, and in writing—because different people learn differently.

The pastor should also select some other key individuals, either from the church board or the planning committee, who have good communication skills and who are wholly sold out to the vision, and delegate to them the shared responsibility of communicating the vision. If the vision has more than one mouthpiece, the feeling begins to grow that the direction of the church is widely shared and it's not just the pastor's pet project.

Effective communication at every stage of the vision-casting, planning, and building process is absolutely essential. Don't take for granted that your people will know what's going on and will support it. Tell them, tell them, and tell them again, and then listen to their feedback. The more interactive you can make the process, the more effective and successful you will be.

Although the pastor should be the primary facilitator for casting the vision, he isn't "the oracle." His role is to facilitate and encourage participation and to provide leadership and guidance but not to control the process. After the core committee has agreed upon a written vision statement, the pastor's role is to carry it forward and be the principle spokesman. If the pastor is wise, he will have been observing the vision-casting committee and will have identified gifted individuals who can communicate effectively, and he will empower them also to promote the vision.

The more people you can involve in the communication process, the broader the appeal to the congregation will be and the less the focus will be on the pastor. If the vision becomes too centered on the pastor, and he decides for some reason to leave, what happens to the vision? Does it leave with him? Not if you've done an effective job of broadcasting the vision to the congregation and fostering widespread support. A well-crafted and widely maintained vision transcends individuals and continues to go forward even if the pastor leaves. If the vision statement truly represents the mission, dreams, and plans of the congregation, the vision won't die just because the pastor leaves.

Your vision statement should reflect the passions and priorities of the congregation, not just the pastor or the board. A compelling vision can become a rallying point for the congregation in terms of the ongoing flow of ministry and the overarching philosophy of ministry, so that when you come to a crossroads and are seeking new pastoral leadership, you can develop a very clear profile of the type of leader for which you are looking—one who won't come in with an entirely new vision. This doesn't mean that a new pastor won't bring his own perspective and impart a freshness to the vision, but a change in leadership should not result in a major turn away from the ongoing mission of the church. If there is a change in leadership, the vision and culture of the church should carry forward essentially intact. There shouldn't be a complete paradigm shift.

Done properly, with widespread congregational representation and involvement, your mission and vision statements will give the congregation a great sense of stability and flow. Who you are, collectively, as a church will be something that's bigger than yourselves, bigger than your pastor, something that God has ordained. You will have a sense of what God desires for your church.

Able, wise, and godly leaders are essential, but God is ultimately in control. If your pastor decides, for whatever reason, to move on, you can be certain that God has prepared another individual who will embrace the church's vision and can lead the congregation forward.

Doing the hard work of articulating in writing the vision for your congregation is not only an essential step in developing the right building, but also a tremendous step toward developing a culture with staying power and momentum and one that can continue to drive toward the goal, even when mid-course changes occur.

If your vision is focused, when you evaluate a given area of ministry, you can either say "that fits, let's do it" or "let's not do that because it doesn't fit who we are." Always test new ideas against the broader vision to ensure that they don't lead you down a rabbit trail away from your primary purpose. If your church is vibrant and growing, there will be no shortage of "great ideas" for ministry, programs, and activities. Everybody and his brother will be pitching in with ideas—and that is exactly what you want. But when it comes time to evaluate these suggestions, one of the first questions should always be, "Does it match our vision?" Is it consistent with what we're here to do? Is it part of where we believe God is calling us to go? If we have agreed that we're not going to be all things to all people, can we support some other ministry to meet that need and allow ourselves to remain focused on the things that God has called us to do?

The Sequence of Vision Sharing

Step one is casting the right vision. Step two is seeding that vision into the congregation—a communication and feedback program that may take up to six months or more to do well. Don't try to rush or shortcut the vision-sharing process. You want your congregation to understand and genuinely support the mission and vision of the church. If you try an end run around your congregation or try to railroad your vision and building plans through, you're courting disaster and disappointment when the time comes to raise your financing and move ahead with the building.

If the congregation does not recognize the need for a vision statement—if you start talking about vision and people say, "Why do we need to do that? Why don't we just keep on doing what we're doing?"—before you can move forward, you probably need two or three teaching times (whether as part of a sermon series or in a separate forum) to help them see the value of vision-casting and to get them used to the idea of thinking in visionary, strategic ways.

The vision-sharing process may reveal that you have not adequately prepared your people for stewardship, commitment, or the proposed direction of the church's ministry. As you go through the SWOT analysis, one of your identified weaknesses might be that you have an underprepared congregation. If that's the case, you will need an action plan to remedy the situation. You might need to develop curriculum, a preaching plan, or some other body of information that will communicate the essential principles that your congregation must learn to support the mission and vision of the church. Again, avoid the temptation to rush the process. God is not in a hurry, so why should you be? Take a long-term perspective. If you're starting from scratch, it might take as much as a year, and certainly no less than six months, to complete the education process. In the meantime, you might have to table your building plans to avoid being manipulative with your teaching.

Why put mission and vision first? Because it's a terrible mistake if you don't. If you don't have a clear vision to guide you, the chances are pretty small that you will accidentally build the ideal building to service all the ministries of the church. Mission and vision have *everything* to do with what your ministry looks like and what your building should look like. And if they don't, it's going to be a disaster—guaranteed.

I know of a church on the West Coast that failed to think through the implications of their vision. Although their ministry was regional in focus, they purchased property in a suburban neighborhood with narrow access streets. The resulting traffic and noise impact on the surrounding community soon had their neighbors up in arms, making for a very unhappy situation. Remember, every decision you make in the building process will have consequences—both intended and unintended—for both the members of your congregation and your neighbors.

Another church wanted to move from its city location out into the country to gain more room for future expansion. They bought some acreage without considering the zoning laws and other issues. When the time came to build, they met resistance from the surrounding landowners who didn't want a church in that location. Eventually, after months of wrangling and trying to work things out, the church had to sell the property—and took a loss when it sold for less than they had paid.

In another situation, a congregation in a Midwestern community failed to articulate a clear vision of their church's ministry strengths. This fuzzy view of their purpose and plan opened them up to the whim of the moment while they were building their new facility. Right in the middle of their construction project, they sensed an "opportunity" to "save some money later" by adding a gymnasium to the current plans.

Unfortunately, they couldn't afford the additional expense, and the problems that resulted from this decision were monumental. It not only completely decimated their financial plan but also caused them to launch a new recreational ministry without adequate staffing or systems to manage the new activities. As a result of this ill-conceived decision, the church soon found itself in serious financial trouble, and their reputation in the community was tarnished by their poorly run programs.

Handling Disagreement or Dissension

What about people who just can't or won't get on board? How does a pastor walk through that minefield? If you've made the vision-casting process collaborative and interactive, and if you've done a consistent and conscientious job of communicating with the congregation at each stage of the operation, one would hope that the resulting vision would be inclusive enough that everyone in the congregation could find elements in it that were compelling. If, despite your best efforts, someone still says, "Well, that's not *my* vision of what a church should be," and he doesn't see how he can support the direction of the church, you must find a graceful way for him to exit without losing face or tearing someone else's face off in the process.

I would advocate using the model of Matthew 18:15–17 for conflict resolution. Start by sitting down with the person one-on-one and asking, "What have we missed in our vision-casting that is keeping you from supporting the vision, or what is it you disagree with concerning what we're trying to accomplish? How can we bring our viewpoints together and reconcile them?" Pray that it won't be necessary, but if your first meeting fails to bring resolution, ask one or two other leaders to join the discussion (per Matt. 18:16), and continue to work toward resolution. If this second phase of mediation is still unsuccessful, ask the dissenter whether he thinks he can stay in the church and support the overall mission despite his disagreement. If not, make clear that if he chooses to leave the church, you will bless him, and if his view of the church's mission ever changes, he will always be welcomed back into your fellowship. Romans 12:18 says, "If possible, as far as it depends on you, be at peace with all men," and, as Romans 14:19 says, "Let us pursue the things which make for peace and the building up of one another."

Be careful to conduct these proceedings in such a way that others don't become unnecessarily involved or that it becomes divisive within the congregation. Don't create waves in the church. Early in the vision-casting process, you would do well to teach your congregation how to resolve conflict biblically (if you haven't done so already), and, if it comes to it, how to leave the church graciously, without creating hard feelings or a backlash.

Because we're all human and walk in the flesh, sometimes we just can't work things out with each other. But how the pastor handles conflict or disagreement over the vision, how he responds, and how he brings leadership to the situation rather than just rebuffing the dissenter will have a lot to do with how the rest of the congregation views the disagreement. Even if someone ultimately chooses to leave the church (and you hope it's not the pastor!)—if the situation has been handled biblically, if the pastor has remained open and available and gentle but wise; and if he has maintained an open, teachable spirit, even if a disagreement remains—those people who are on the periphery observing the process should be able to say, "It's unfortunate that our dissenting brother couldn't see it, but the pastor certainly responded well." If, on the other hand, you end up with two immovable forces bashing each other, then everybody loses. No matter what happens, remember that relationships are primary in God's economy. Do everything you can to preserve peace and fellowship.

Overcoming Obstacles to Consensus

How does a congregation overcome its weaknesses and threats and take advantage of its strengths and opportunities to get to its desired future? It might be through change that is very uncomfortable for some people because they're averse to debt or because they recognize that the church needs $500,000 to achieve its goals and it's going to cost everyone some blood, sweat, and tears. It might require a change in the way the church budgets and allocates its resources.

Here is where "buy-in" to the vision becomes crucial for removing major stumbling blocks. As soon as you start talking about dollars and cents, everyone who wasn't entirely sold on the vision will come out of the woodwork and say, "What if it doesn't work? What if we spend this $500,000 and people still don't come?" In other words, what if Kevin Costner had built the field of dreams and the old ballplayers didn't come? At times like these, the leaders and the congregation must decide how strongly they believe in the articulation of the vision and the plans that have been set in place to reach that vision. If the commitment to the vision is strong, then the naysayers and "what iffers" won't be able to derail the process or discourage the people. On the other hand, if the commitment is soft or tentative, then you're dead in the water because the first guy who says "What if . . . ?" will knock the wind out of everyone's sails.

I can guarantee that the second-guessers will surface when you start talking dollars and cents because it touches their pocketbooks. That's why you want to try to identify the fence straddlers during the vision-casting process, so you can draw them in and involve them in the process as early as possible. You'll either be able to answer their concerns up front or at least get them on board enough that they can't stand up and say "What if . . . ?" without feeling foolish. If they're part of the decision-making process, they can't come back later and say, "I told you so." Furthermore, if you can build a broad coalition right from the start, it lessens your chances of missing the target by a mile.

Regardless of whether your church is governed by a board of elders or deacons or every major decision must go before the congregation, it's important to have some mechanism in place to measure the level of commitment among the people *before* the issue comes up for a vote. Soliciting feedback—and *listening* to it—is absolutely essential to effective communication. Be honest with yourself. Have you built consensus? Is there a sense of shared need? Do the majority of people recognize that you need to do something about the nursery, or is it just two very vocal mothers? I'm not discounting the perspective of one or two individuals, but for your building project to move forward, you must build a consensus that incorporates a significant majority of the congregation. Otherwise, you can fall prey to vocal special interest groups and the pressure can begin to build. If it happens that one of the vocal people is a very significant contributor to the general fund, the leverage increases. Before you know it, the entire process can be sidetracked or railroaded by an influential minority.

Changing to Stay the Same

No matter how rapidly the project moves along, it is always important to keep the vision fresh and keep people focused on where you're headed and how you're progressing. Obviously, the longer the timeline, the more important it is to keep bringing people back to the vision. It is so easy to get off on the issues of the day and lose sight of the ultimate goal.

When I was an associate pastor with a church in California, it took us six years after we acquired land—and seven years total—actually to build the building and move into it. During that time, we continually had to refresh the vision with architectural pictures of the buildings, four-wheel-drive trips up to the site, groundbreaking ceremonies—all kinds of things—to keep us focused on the goal. We talked about becoming "God's light set on the hill" because our new site was above the valley we were serving.

Even if you have a ministry or program that everyone agrees is well focused, well executed, and successful, you must keep an eye on it and periodically review your vision, strategies, and action plans to maintain your consistency.

Maintaining consistency is one of the hallmarks of the Krispy

Kreme doughnut company. According to Charles Fishman, a contributing editor for FastCompany.com, Krispy Kreme "is so obsessed with consistency that before each batch of wheat flour is allowed into the building, a sample is tested in a second-floor lab. . . . If a 25-ton truckload of flour falls outside of established parameters, the entire delivery is rejected. . . . Adjacent to the lab is a full-scale doughnut-making kitchen . . . [where] baking lab technicians . . . make doughnuts from every single 2,500-pound batch of mix, making sure that each batch has been blended correctly."

Over the years, Krispy Kreme's doughnut mix has been adjusted and no longer matches the original recipe, but the quality of the finished product has remained consistent. Mike Cecil, Krispy Kreme's "minister of culture" explains: "Modern cooking equipment, the size of the company, and the vagaries of the wheat crop all require adjustments. The recipe has to change for the doughnuts to stay the same."

If you want to keep your ministry consistent with your vision in the face of an ever-changing environment, you will occasionally need to tinker with the mix. For example, you might need to review and periodically revise how you deal with youth ministries. As the needs of growing families ebb and flow, you might need to tweak your nursery program or beef up your Sunday school or other components of your ministry. Usually, strategies and action plans will have to change to maintain consistency.

If you keep the emphasis on the ministry aspects of the mission and vision, it's easier to keep people focused during the preconstruction and building processes. Remember that you're not just building a building; you're developing a tool, a facility, to enhance the effective ministry of the church.

Keeping the Vision Fresh

Keeping the vision alive is a matter of effective communication. Always start with your core constituents, the people who are most committed and most familiar with the vision, and keep working out in concentric circles until you get to the edges where you're trying to impart the vision to those who are new and just coming in.

Having some sort of a new members' process is important. This way, as people come into your fellowship, they are taken through an introduction to the ministry of the church (the doctrine, how the church functions, the ministries, etc.). At the same time, they ought to be introduced to the vision, the master plan, the phases of development, and where the church is on the continuum.

Every time you have a business meeting or an annual meeting, it's very important to discuss the vision and refocus the congregation's attention on the goals and action plans. Everyone should be brought up to date on how the church is progressing toward its goals, and time should be allowed for questions and answers. On such occasions, you want to invite discussion and interaction. As long as everyone is aware that the vision is a work in progress and not something etched in stone, no one should feel the need to become defensive about it. Encouraging open discussion is a great way to build a sense of ownership of the process throughout the congregation.

Maintain the vision, adjust it as you go, and communicate progress reports throughout the system. Then, as each successive phase comes along, it's not a surprise; in fact, each new phase should generate renewed excitement as people see the vision gradually coming to life.

My belief is that planning for your next building project should be a normal outgrowth of a continual focus on the future and your vision. You're always dealing with where you are today, but you have your mind's eye on where you believe the Lord is leading your congregation in the future.

Bringing the Vision to Life

You will never accomplish all that God has for your church if you don't exercise the discipline to articulate the vision clearly and define the desired results. As you look out at your community, ask yourself, "How are we going to reach them?" Start with a season of prayer; then, as the Lord leads, supplement your prayer by getting out into the community to uncover the needs—both actual and felt. If you are going to be deliberate and intentional about accomplishing the vision God has given you, one of your early action steps has to be research.

Throughout the process, continually come back to the mission and vision to keep your bearings. Revise the plan as you grow, but never lose sight of the underlying purpose, which should remain constant. Align your action steps with the natural rhythms of life and ministry. After completing a phase, every congregation needs time to breathe, recover, and celebrate what has been accomplished. A very significant part of body life is keeping the vision fresh and alive without drowning people in it. Don't be in such a hurry to reach the finish line that you trample your people in the process.

Vision is always a work in progress. At least annually you should be refreshing the vision and adjusting your ministry plan. Ask yourself, your leaders, and your members, "What have we learned about ourselves this year? Is our vision too big or too small?" As you review your successes and your challenges, ask, "Where does this leave us on our continuum and what new issues are we facing? What should we be doing this year? Where should our primary focus be?"

Until the Lord returns, we never finish working on our vision; we never finish developing our strategic plans. We're always growing because we're always learning. We pray, devise our plans, work out our action steps, and learn as we go—then pray, revise, and work some more. That's vision in action.

Chapter 4

STEWARDSHIP: PUTTING KINGDOM DOLLARS TO WORK

ONCE THE VISION IS set and you have defined your needs, wants, and dreams, you should have some idea of the type of building you will need. The next logical question is, "How are we going to pay for all of this?"

The answer depends in part on the financial strength of your congregation, their understanding of stewardship, and your philosophy of debt. Before you start spending a lot of money on master plans and blueprints, you should assess both your current financial capacity and how you anticipate your growth to occur so that you can reasonably project your ability to accomplish your vision. That doesn't mean that you don't trust God to supply your needs as you go along, but it does mean that you count the cost before you begin. "For which one of you, when he wants to build a tower, does not first sit down and calculate the cost, to see if he has enough to complete it? Otherwise, when he has laid a foundation, and is not able to finish, all who observe it begin to ridicule him, saying, 'This man began to build and was not able to finish'" (Luke 14:28–30).

To determine your congregation's current ability to achieve its objectives, start by establishing a budget based on current finances and your potential for borrowing. A sound budget will set boundaries around the development of your list of needs, wants, and desires.

Start with a Solid Financial Plan

If you're serious about growing, expanding, and building your church, you'll want to prepare a financial plan right from the beginning. Wise stewardship takes into consideration God's ability to provide resources, as well as your congregation's established pattern of giving. It's important to look at your church's financial performance (past and present), study the trends, look at per capita giving, and evaluate how well your congregation has accepted the challenge of supporting God's work financially. This is also a good time to estimate your borrowing capability in case the size of your project exceeds your current cash reserves.

At the end of the chapter, we have included the following materials to help you get a handle on your congregation's financial strength: *(a)* "A Simple Church Budget," *(b)* "Calculating Your Monthly Payment," and *(c)* "Calculating Debt to Value Ratio." Take the time to work through these forms with your leadership team.

If you don't take stock of financial reality, you can do all of the dreaming, vision-casting, and planning you want only to realize that there's no way you can afford your plans. Although finances should never dictate the vision, your finances must be in balance with the vision, or they will harpoon the vision—guaranteed. One of the quickest ways to demoralize a core leadership team is for the bottom to fall out of the finances and the project to grind to a halt. When that happens, all of the momentum dissipates, the focus is lost, and everybody starts pointing fingers—usually at the pastor.

A tragic story occurred in a Midwestern church where, halfway through the building project, the leadership team strayed from their vision and plan and increased the size of the building without counting the cost. The net result was that the building was never finished, the property was eventually foreclosed, and the church had to relocate.

In another situation, a church in the Northwest retained an architect and embarked on the planning phase of their building project before they had established their budget. When the initial design came back, it called for a building that went well beyond the amount they could truly afford. Unfortunately, by the time they figured out their budgetary shortfall, they had already become emotionally connected with the design. They decided to move ahead but then had to scramble to put together a financing plan to meet the contract they had signed. Sadly, the church is now overextended and struggling to make its monthly payments while trying to maintain their existing ministry programs.

Budgetary shortfalls are almost always a precursor to significant struggles for a congregation. It is absolutely essential to evaluate your ability to pay and to plan your construction project accordingly so that you are able to bring your project to completion without difficulty or dissension.

Your Vision and God's Provision

I don't believe that God would give your church a vision without providing the means to attain it. If you're lacking financially, why? Is it because the pastor hasn't done enough teaching about the responsibilities and benefits of tithing? Is it because your leaders have not communicated the vision well enough that it's compelling? Has the process been bathed in prayer so you're confident that the plans you have devised are the Lord's plans? What steps do you need to take as a congregation over the next six months to address a biblical view of church finances? As a leader, what do you need to do differently to inform your congregation adequately about the role of stewardship in accomplishing the vision of the church so they can make the decision of whether to get on board?

As a pastoral leader, you have a responsibility to teach the whole counsel of God, to rightly divide the word of truth. That includes talking about giving. Unfortunately, a majority of the pastoral leaders in America never talk about money because they think they'll be characterized as always trying to reach into people's pockets. Baloney! Teach the biblical principles. Don't add to them, don't take away from them, don't water them down, and don't overhype them. Don't place a burden of guilt on your congregation; just teach the biblical principles, allow the Holy Spirit to minister, and let your people make decisions for themselves and their families about how they're going to respond. Take God at His Word. He is faithful. Don't rob your people of the blessing that comes through giving back to God financially.

Planning for Success—or Failure?

Everything we've discussed to this point assumes that you are building on the solid foundation of a ministry plan that has its roots in a clearly defined mission and vision. Once the foundation has been established, there's a tremendous amount of wisdom in simply "doing the ministry" day in and day out, working the plan and walking through the process. That's the hard work of the ministry. Unfortunately, a lot of pastors aren't willing or able to discipline themselves to do the hard work. It isn't always fun to look ahead to the next twelve Sundays and ask yourself, "What are the core principles that must be articulated during this next season? Am I going to preach through Joshua, Romans, or Matthew? How am I going to articulate fully God's Word in good, solid teaching?"

Every component of your ministry, from teaching to preaching to activities, should support the mission and the vision of the church; otherwise, why are you doing it? I get nervous when pastors don't have well-conceived plans. Some pastors give the impression that they're waiting for Saturday night to see what the Lord lays on their hearts. The danger in not having a systematic ministry plan is that you're almost guaranteed to wander away from the vision and skip over important truths in your teaching. And when the time comes to build, you're likely to find out that your congregation is unprepared to move ahead with the plan.

If you haven't been teaching your congregation about biblical giving as a regular and normal part of your ministry plan, you're robbing them of an opportunity to receive a blessing from God and to be a part of something bigger than what they have ever dreamed. On the other hand, if you've focused sufficient attention on communicating the vision of the church and have explained the financial realities that accompany the vision, I'm convinced that when the time comes to move ahead, the dollars will be available to do what you want to do.

God's Plan in God's Time

Timing is a very important factor. One of the hardest things to do is wait—to discipline yourself to hold out for God's perfect timing and not to come up with your own clever plans for how to get things done. On the other hand, it's easy to use the refrain "We're waiting on God" as an excuse for not doing what you can to prepare and plan. Once you've done your homework in vision-casting, budgeting, and planning; once you've laid the groundwork by teaching the necessary biblical principles; and once you've properly articulated a clear and compelling vision and your congregation has begun to rally around that vision, one of the simplest ways to determine whether you're in God's timing is to look at the budget. Have faith promise pledges started showing up in the offering plate? Has giving to the general fund maintained its course or even increased in anticipation of upcoming needs? Have designated gifts begun filling up the building fund? It still might not be God's timing (remember John Maxwell's story in the introduction about the "perfect" thirty-acre parcel that God kept them from buying), but as the pieces begin to fall into place, you can pray for God to reveal His wisdom for specific decisions about timing, location, and financing.

If you've diligently taught your congregation the full counsel of Scripture, and if you've involved them in casting the vision for the church so that they can embrace and support its goals and directions, they'll already know what it means to give sacrificially, they'll know when they're feeling the Lord prompt them to commit themselves, and they'll be willing to move ahead. Far too often, though, when the timing is delayed, it's because the groundwork has not been properly put in place, the necessary information has not been imparted to the congregation, or the financial realities have not been communicated adequately. The end result is that people feel manipulated and coerced into financing a vision they neither embrace nor fully understand. Coerced commitments are not spiritual commitments, and spiritual commitments are not coerced.

Even before you sit down to do your vision-casting, you really should commit to a season of prayer in the church in anticipation of setting the future course for the congregation and to ask for the Lord's direction for the whole process—and especially to keep everything aboveboard and nonmanipulative. And then prayer should prevail throughout the process. Every meeting should begin with prayer. Be intentional about it, and pray for specific elements throughout the process.

Proper stewardship is a very delicate balance. On the one hand, you shouldn't be reluctant to ask people to sacrifice. My personal view is that it's good for them. But sacrificial giving needs to be something born in the spirit by the Spirit and not as the consequence of feeling pressured by man.

Spiritual commitments are born out of genuine convictions and are focused on a vision to reach people with the gospel and influence the direction of their lives. Spiritual commitments don't come from having your arm leveraged behind your back until you cry "uncle." If the pastor dusts off his "stewardship sermon" only when it's time to raise money for something, if it's not a regular part of body life and connected to the church's vibrant vision, then your members will inevitably feel that they are knuckling under to strong-arm tactics, and they will end up feeling negative about both the project and the pastor.

Another issue that can create negative feelings within the congregation is disagreement over the proper use of credit and outside financing. Part of the controversy results from a misapplication of personal financial principles to the corporate entity of the church.

Is Debt Unholy?

A number of Christian financial advisors have written some wonderful books to help individuals gain control of their finances and spending. Although I agree with many of the principles that they present, I believe it's a mistake to apply them directly to the church as though they were directly transferable—because they're not. Unfortunately, a lot of churches try to operate according to a "personal finances" model, to the detriment of their ministries.

One such principle that many financial advisors recommend, but with which I disagree, is the idea that we should pay down the mortgage to "get out of debt." In my view, the church is to be focused on ministry, not on the dubious security that comes from having the building paid off. How does paying off the mortgage serve the mission or vision of the church? The mission of the church is to reach the lost and dying in its community with the good news of salvation in Jesus Christ and to disciple its congregation into fully mature members of the body of Christ.

The stewardship responsibilities of a church and individuals are also very different. Unlike an individual or a family, the church is a nonprofit corporation that must function in a biblically sound way in the business world. As a corporate entity, the church has different capabilities and different responsibilities than does an individual. It has a different mission. And the church, because it is an aggregate body, has a lot more financial strength than does an individual or a family.

A more apt model of comparison for how the church should

manage its resources might be a manufacturing or service business. In a factory, for example, deciding to pay off the mortgage on the building and equipment instead of using the same revenue to purchase raw materials to produce more product—or, in the case of a service business, to pay off the building rather than to hire more sales representatives and service technicians—makes about as much sense as a church's paying off its mortgage instead of investing those same assets more effectively in expanding its ministry both at home and abroad. The key issue is which allocation of resources best serves and advances the mission and vision of the organization.

What Is Debt?

One subject on which I disagree with many Christian financial advisors is that of debt. Some financial planners define *debt* as "anytime you borrow" or "anytime you owe anything to anybody." Based on that premise, they'll take a verse such as Romans 13:8, "Owe nothing to anyone except to love one another," and suggest that borrowing money is wrong. I disagree. "Borrowing money" and "being in debt" are not the same thing. From my perspective, you are not in debt unless one or more of the following conditions applies:

1. you owe more than you own (i.e., you have no equity),
2. the cash flow requirements are greater than you can manage, or
3. you are delinquent in your payments.

If any of these three conditions apply, then you are in debt. But if you've simply borrowed $200,000, for example, to purchase a $400,000 building, and you can comfortably manage the $1800 monthly payment from your current cash flow or revenue, from my perspective you are not in debt because you have equity in the building and could liquidate the asset at any time to repay what you owe.

Based on the preceding definition of debt, I would agree that churches should avoid going into debt. The best way to avoid debt is to establish sufficient equity in the asset you are purchasing so that the payments are manageable and you never owe more than the asset is worth. If a church is going to erect a building, my first question is, "How much cash do you have in your building fund to put into the project?"

If the pastor says, "Well, we're going to borrow the money, so we don't need a building fund," my next question is, "Where is your equity going to come from?" No lender is going to loan 100 percent of the value of the building. You need to establish at least a 20 percent equity position to qualify for a loan, and only two ways exist to build equity: cash or sweat labor.

On top of that, you need to figure out how you're going to make your payments. As you look at your general fund—the total revenue of the church, excluding missions or other restricted gifts—a standard rule of thumb is that you can afford to pay 30–33 percent of net revenue to meet a mortgage obligation.

Let's say that your general fund receipts average $10,000 per month. According to recognized lending-industry standards, you can afford to commit about $3,000 per month (30–33%) of that $10,000 to make your mortgage payment, which means that, depending on the prevailing interest rate, you can afford about a $300,000–$350,000 mortgage. If the mortgage represents no more than 80 percent of the value of the building (which must be true for you to qualify for the loan), then you can afford a building that would cost $375,000–$450,000, and you would need to raise $75,000–$100,000 in cash to establish an equity stake greater than 20 percent and keep your mortgage below $350,000.

If the value of your proposed building is $450,000 and you've raised $100,000 in cash to put into the project, as long as you make your regular monthly payments and the market value remains steady or moves up by at least the rate of inflation, you're establishing an increasing equity position in your building.

Although you owe the bank $350,000, from my perspective that isn't debt; that's good stewardship because you're meeting your need for a new building without having to sacrifice ministry to do it. If, on the other hand, you insist on raising the full $450,000 in cash before you start to build, how much other ministry will you have to forego in the meantime, and what will happen to the cost of construction while you are salting away the cash to pay for your project? A wise steward counts all of the costs before he begins to build.

What happens, though, if you need to service a $300,000 mortgage but your general fund is running at $8,000 per month instead of $10,000? At that rate, the $3,000 monthly payment would be higher than 33 percent of your monthly revenue. If you are unable to scale back your building project to a level that you can afford from your current giving, my approach would be to go to the congregation and say, "We need faith promise commitments to supplement our general fund by $2,000 a month for (let's say) three years, until we can grow to the place where our general fund will support our mortgage obligation." I believe that is a reasonable approach to the problem. You can use certain mechanisms to arrange your finances such that you can make it through. Again, this is all part of counting the cost before you begin.

Should the Church Be Debt Free?

To avoid becoming entangled in semantics, let's make one thing clear right now. If you accept my definition of *debt* (which occurs only if you owe more than you own, you cannot manage the payments from your cash flow, or you are delinquent in your payments), then we can agree that being "debt free" is the only way to fly. Clearly, if the alternative is being upside down financially, it's obvious why you would want to avoid debt. On the other hand, some people in your congregation (and you might be one of them) will insist that being "debt free" means that the church should operate on a straight cash basis with no outstanding obligations. From my perspective, this definition of "debt free" is shortsighted and not necessarily biblical.

If I had a church board that was saying, "We want to double or triple our mortgage payments until we're debt free," my immediate question would be, "Why? What is behind the drive to be debt free?" If your motivation for paying off the mortgage is security, I have to ask you, "Where is your security, in your building or in the Lord?" If your security is in the Lord, then what is the highest and best use of the dollars that He's entrusted to you as stewards? Is it to pay off the mortgage, or is it to make your monthly payments and use the difference to start a youth program or a meal program for the poor or to fund a missions trip to Nicaragua? What can you do that will be effective ministry, will move your congregation toward achieving its vision, and will be consistent with your mission statement? Whatever it is, spend your available dollars there. I believe that pastors have a responsibility to lead their congregations into a balanced view of borrowing and an optimal use of the dollars that are flowing in. Let's have an impact on people's lives, not just the loan department of a bank.

In my view, the scariest day in the life of a church is the day they burn the mortgage. Unless they have a compelling vision of the future that will continue to pull them forward, the danger in "finally paying everything off" is that the church will settle back and become complacent, and the congregation will become averse to taking on new obligations and fresh challenges. If you've ever walked into an outdated sanctuary or an old church fellowship hall or Sunday school classroom, then you know what I'm talking about. I've seen it happen time and again: a church pays off its mortgage, loses its edge, loses its forward-looking perspective, and begins an inevitable decline.

Now, don't get me wrong. Paying off the mortgage doesn't cause the problem. It's what happens next—either putting those available dollars to work or resting on the church's laurels—that sets the course for continued growth or decline. If I were still a pastor and my church was "debt free," I'd be looking for a project. It might be planting a church in another community, adding a building to our facility, creating a new outreach ministry in our neighborhood or town, or starting a progressive renovation and updating of our present building. I'd be looking for a project to put the church's underused assets to work. Like the two wise stewards in Jesus' parable of the talents (Matt. 25:14–30), I'd be looking for a way to maximize the return on our available resources.

The Cost of Paying Cash

One argument I've heard against borrowing is that "I don't want to pay interest. That's money down a rat hole. We could use those dollars for ministry." True, but when? If you're doubling payments to the bank or socking away a huge war chest so you can "build for cash," when will you be able to use those dollars for ministry? Why not finance your new building and use the capital that those dollars represent for ministry right now? The straight cost of financing is not the only expense to consider. What about the opportunity cost of tying up the church's resources to buy down the existing mortgage, or trying to accumulate a 100 percent building fund? Lost opportunities in ministry are seldom recovered.

Although I would agree that a church should keep its interest expense to a minimum (don't pay any more than necessary), paying interest is not inherently evil. If you work with a bank that you respect, is it a problem that its shareholders benefit by earning interest on your loan? Now, if they're also financing construction of an adult bookstore down the street from your church, that might be a little different situation. That's where denominational resources such as the Church Extension Plan can have an edge because all of the money we take in is redirected into church loans. We don't do anything else. If you can use a denominational resource, where all of the interest is invested in other church loans, then the argument against paying interest is eliminated because they're all kingdom dollars at that point.

An appropriate use of borrowing balances outstanding obligations against the constraints of the budget so that you're not compromising ministry in favor of paying off your loans, nor are you underusing available resources that could be used to pay for additional ministries. The object is to leverage your use of borrowed funds such that you accomplish the goals of your mission and vision without ending up in debt (according to our definition). I am not advocating that a church go out and borrow more than is reasonable or necessary, but neither should you avoid borrowing just because it creates a financial obligation.

Never Mortgage the Future

Another key principle of wise stewardship is that you work with what you have today, not with what you think you might have tomorrow. Never say, "Well, with this new facility we'll be able to grow from one hundred members to three hundred, and at three hundred we'll be able to afford the payment, so we can borrow that much." Always start with where you are; otherwise, you put an awful lot of pressure on your congregation to grow to three hundred (or whatever the number is in your case), and if it doesn't happen, then you're upside down financially. I have seen far too many churches try to stretch beyond a reasonable level—and they end up paying for it in the long run. Always plan and borrow based on what you can afford today. It might mean that you have to complete your project in phases because you can't afford to do everything today that needs to be done. You always have to bring your present vision back to the realities of the budget, but never mortgage the future.

Don't Overlook Ongoing Expenses

When you're figuring out how much monthly expense you can afford, don't forget to include the cost of maintenance in your calculations. Depending on the size of your church—both the building and the congregation—upkeep on your facility might have significant budgetary ramifications. It might be necessary and wise to establish cash reserves to pay for eventual big-ticket maintenance, such as a new roof or new paint, and don't overlook regular and ongoing expenses such as replacing furnace filters and light bulbs. If it costs $100 per calendar quarter to replace furnace filters, for example, and you haven't budgeted the money to do it so you don't replace the filters, you could end up spending $2000 for a new compressor. The reality is that the more you defer maintenance because "we don't have the cash right now," the more it will cost later, and the more damage that might be done that will require further investment.

Decide whether you're going to reserve cash or simply allocate for maintenance expenses each year in the budget (as a maintenance or capital improvement line item). Make your decisions based on a clear understanding of your church's cash flow and how it will work best for your fellowship. You're far better off to plan maintenance expenses into your budget right from the start, and do the work progressively as it comes up rather than letting upkeep slide. The time to make those decisions is during the planning process, not after the building is completed.

When Is It Wise to Stretch?

Once you have a firm idea of what is affordable, you can evaluate specific opportunities where it might make sense to stretch a little—those situations where for a few dollars more you can make a major step forward. For example, let's say that your church is buying a five-acre parcel, which fits your near-term plan and your present budget, but for 25 percent more you could purchase ten acres. And when you look at your master plan and your future vision, the ten acres really makes a lot more sense from a long-term perspective. Is that a time to stretch a little bit? Would it make sense to pull in a little bit on the rest of your budget and stretch to cover the extra 25 percent—thereby opening your horizons for the future? Probably so. Of course, your next question should be, "What must we do within our budget to make room for the stretching?"

Every situation will be different, and there are many other factors to consider, but if your vision is clear, compelling, and comprehensive, and if you've done a good job of evaluating your financial capabilities, you are in a position to make a wise and prudent decision about a specific opportunity that comes along. Instead of scrambling around in the dark and risking an unwise decision, you will be prepared to ask yourself a few very specific questions, including the following.

- Do we need the additional acreage to accomplish our vision?
- How soon will we need it? Could we sub-lease the property in the meantime to help defray the additional cost?
- What impact will the additional cost have on the budget?
- Do we have funds available within the current budget without diminishing our capacity for ministry, or should (can) we raise that money separately?
- Is this a strategic moment when a slight stretch will help us reach our vision? (If so, you can usually rally people around the revised vision and get the job done.)

The bottom line is always "What can we really afford?" and "What does it mean to our plan?" If you've laid the proper groundwork, your vision statement ought to set the mileposts out there. My hope is that your vision will not only cause you to think big but also allow you to avoid overreaching.

Another advantage of a clear vision statement is that it allows you to develop a sense of pace. With a good plan in place, every new decision doesn't create a crisis. Instead, you're able to approach this journey with the confidence that you don't need to get to the finish line in the next ten seconds. You know where you're headed, that it's a journey, and that you have time to get there. As with any gradual process, you need to crawl before you can walk before you can run.

A Simple Church Budget

Guidelines for Developing an Annual Church Budget
A budget is a roadmap for you to use to advance toward your ministry's vision. Drawing from last year's expenses and your current goals, you can develop a picture of what to expect for the coming year. Getting input from heads of your various departments that are affected by the budget will be very beneficial in developing an accurate picture of your church's financial plan.

	DETAIL	SUBTOTAL	CATEGORY SUBTOTAL
ANTICIPATED REVENUE *(One Year)*			
General Fund (Tithe/Offering)	$ _____		
Missions	_____		
Christian Education	_____		
Building Fund	_____		
Designated Funds	_____		
Special Offerings	_____		
Rental Revenue	_____		
Other	_____		
TOTAL ANNUAL REVENUE			$ _____
ANTICIPATED EXPENSES *(One Year)*			
Personnel			
Salaries	$ _____		
Insurance	_____		
Housing and Utilities	_____		
Transportation	_____		
Social Security/Retirement	_____		
District and General Council Meetings	_____		
Continuing Education and Training	_____		
Other	_____		
TOTAL PERSONNEL		$ _____	

	DETAIL	SUBTOTAL	CATEGORY SUBTOTAL

World Ministries

Foreign Missions	$_____		
Home Missions	_____		
Missions Convention	_____		
Shared Responsibility	_____		
Other	_____		
TOTAL WORLD MINISTRIES		$_____	

Specialized Ministries

Men's Ministry	$_____		
Women's Ministry	_____		
Youth Ministry	_____		
Royal Rangers	_____		
Missionettes	_____		
Summer/Winter Camps	_____		
Music Ministry	_____		
Benevolence	_____		
Advertising (radio, TV, newspaper)	_____		
Other	_____		
TOTAL SPECIALIZED MINISTRIES		$_____	

Christian Education

C.E. Materials	$_____		
Equipment	_____		
Convert Training/Discipleship	_____		
Evangelism Outreach	_____		
Church Library	_____		
Vacation Bible School	_____		
Other	_____		
TOTAL CHRISTIAN EDUCATION		$_____	

Building and Equipment

Utilities	$_____		
Debt Reduction	_____		
Building Maintenance	_____		
Parking Maintenance	_____		
Grounds Maintenance	_____		
Vehicle Fuel/Maintenance	_____		
Sound Equipment/Maintenance	_____		
Insurance	_____		

	DETAIL	SUBTOTAL	CATEGORY SUBTOTAL
Kitchen Equipment	_____		
Other	_____		
TOTAL BUILDING AND EQUIPMENT		$ _____	

Church Office

	DETAIL	SUBTOTAL	
Office Equipment	$_____		
Materials and Supplies	_____		
Bulletins/Mailings	_____		
Postage	_____		
Other	_____		
TOTAL CHURCH OFFICE		$ _____	

Designated Funds

	DETAIL	SUBTOTAL	
Vehicle Acquisition	$_____		
Furnace/Air Conditioning	_____		
Roof	_____		
Carpet	_____		
Sound Equipment/Music Instruments	_____		
Paint (interior/exterior)	_____		
Business Machines (computer, phone/fax, etc.)	_____		
Other	_____		
TOTAL DESIGNATED FUNDS		$ _____	

TOTAL ANNUAL EXPENSES $ _____

NET FUNDS (Revenue — Expenses) $ _____

Summary:

1. Add each Anticipated Revenue detail line to arrive at Total Annual Revenue.
2. Add each Anticipated Expenses detail line to arrive at Subtotals. Add each Anticipated Expenses Subtotal to arrive at Total Annual Expenses.
3. Subtract Total Annual Expenses from Total Annual Revenue. This equals your Net Funds.
4. If revenues exceed expenses, consider using additional funds for debt retirement or major acquisitions.

After a general budget is completed, your next step may be to create an annual budget for each category or department with revenues and expenses recorded month-to-date and year-to-date.

Calculating Your Monthly Payment

	Percentage Rate									
	7%		8%		9%		10%		12%	
Amount Borrowed	20 years	30 years	20 years	30 years	20 years	30 years	20 years	30 years	20 years	30 years
100,000	775	665	836	734	900	805	965	878	1,101	1,029
200,000	1,551	1,331	1,673	1,468	1,799	1,609	1,930	1,755	2,202	2,057
300,000	2,326	1,996	2,509	2,201	2,699	2,414	2,895	2,633	3,303	3,086
400,000	3,101	2,661	3,346	2,935	3,599	3,218	3,860	3,510	4,404	4,114
500,000	3,876	3,327	4,182	3,669	4,499	4,023	4,825	4,388	5,505	5,143
600,000	4,652	3,992	5,019	4,403	5,398	4,828	5,790	5,265	6,607	6,172
700,000	5,427	4,657	5,855	5,136	6,298	5,632	6,755	6,143	7,708	7,200
800,000	6,202	5,322	6,692	5,870	7,198	6,437	7,720	7,021	8,809	8,229
900,000	6,978	5,988	7,528	6,604	8,098	7,242	8,685	7,898	9,90:	9,258
1,000,000	7,753	6,653	8,364	7,338	8,997	8,046	9,650	8,776	11,011	10,286

Calculating Debt-to-Value Ratio

Simple Equation: Amount Borrowed divided by Property Value

Example: A church takes out a loan for $850,000 and the building is valued at $1,200,000

$850,000 divided by $1,200,000 = 70.83% debt-to-value

less than 60% debt-to-value ratio   CONSERVATIVE
60%–85% debt-to-value ratio   AGGRESSIVE
85%–100% debt-to-value ratio   RISKY

Chapter 5

FINDING YOUR FINANCING

THERE ARE NUMEROUS ways to put together a financing package to complete your building project with both integrity and fiscal accountability. I've seen that most people have not only a preferred method, but also their biases as well. I must admit that I carry some biases because of my long involvement in the stewardship area of providing financing for the local church. Sadly, individuals and organizations exist in each sector of the financing industry that function based more upon expediency and "doing the deal" than on what is best for a congregation and its leadership.

My intent in this chapter is not to degrade one method of church financing in favor of another or to attempt to look into the motivation that drives a particular organization or industry group. Rather, I give some general insights about each of the available alternatives and allow you to select the one that best fits your situation. The reality is that no perfect, one-size-fits-all approach to construction financing exists, but there is a way that will best match your congregation's principles and attitudes about borrowing and fundraising.

The success or failure of a given financing option depends upon the particular culture of a congregation. For example, if your members are accustomed to faith-promise giving and offerings over and above the usual tithe, then a capital gift drive may, in some circumstances, fit your congregation more closely than it would another. If, on the other hand, the topic of personal giving is seldom—if ever—raised, then attempting a capital gift campaign might prove to be pure folly. If your congregation has had a bad experience with, or has a cultural aversion to, borrowing money and paying interest, then the idea of financing a building program through a bank loan might be anathema, whereas for another congregation it would be the normal and expected way. It is essential for you and those who advise you to understand the particular culture and expectations of your congregation before presuming to propose a financing plan. What might be a transcendent experience for one congregation might feel like near-death for another.

With that information as a backdrop, let me shed some light on several alternative approaches to financing. Clearly, the size of your building project will have a tremendous impact on the method you choose for your financing plan. For example, if you are doing a relatively minor remodeling project, it might be possible to pay for it out of your general fund offerings or a specific project-based fund-raising appeal. However, if your project involves a major remodeling or construction of a new building of substantial size for your congregation, an organized capital campaign, a bond program, or some other form of capital financing likely will be necessary. Once you have the scope of the project in mind and have developed a keen awareness of the culture of your particular fellowship, you can line up the alternatives and see which one best fits your needs.

Following is the basic list of options:

- an internally generated bond program;
- a bond program organized through an outside provider, consultant, or underwriter;
- a commercial bank loan;
- a loan from a denominational resource;
- a capital fund drive; and
- a "pay-as-you-go" construction plan.

Generally speaking, these options fall into three primary categories: capital campaigns (either internally or externally managed), pay-as-you-go programs, and borrowing from an outside source (a commercial bank, denominational resource, bond program, or other similar mechanism).

Capital Campaigns

A capital campaign is a fund-raising strategy whereby a church establishes a budget and a building fund and then raises the targeted dollars over an extended period of time—say three years, for example. The philosophy behind a capital campaign is that it is wise to build up your war chest before you go to battle. If you start far enough in advance, and if your vision is sufficiently compelling to motivate your congregation to invest the building funds up front, then a capital campaign can work. Unfortunately, in my experience, many churches don't have enough foresight to start the stewardship campaign early enough. Inevitably, they end up trying to erect the building while they are still raising the money. They might use a bridge loan or some other intermediate financial device to get through the process, but this "safety net" can be very costly. On occasion, intermediate financing can be disastrous if the budgeted money doesn't come in.

In a capital stewardship campaign, a church hires a professional fund-raising company to come in and assess the congregation's ability to give. The consultant will generally base his projections on the church's historical giving and attendance records. Then, for a fee, which usually amounts to 6 or 7 percent of the building fund budget, plus printing and travel expenses, the campaign company will train a "stewardship team" from among the church membership to go out and canvass the congregation and secure commitments to donate the money. This approach generally involves a process whereby a steering committee or capital drive team is trained to communicate strategically with the congregation, to generate sacrificial gifts through a prayer and commitment campaign. Frequently, the steering committee is drawn from among the ranks of members who are already significant financial contributors, and often part of the program is to ask the committee members to make substantial commitments so that when the congregation is finally approached, a considerable portion of the funding has already been committed. In many congregations a capital campaign is a reasonable strategy, but it must fit your particular situation.

One of the more crucial elements in a successful capital campaign is establishing an appropriate target. I personally have no problem with a campaigner who suggests that a church seek to raise one and one-half to two times its general fund over a three-year period. I become concerned, however, when the goal stretches to three or three and one-half times the general fund over that same period. Do the math. If you are setting a target to raise three times the value of your current general fund over three years, in essence you are saying that you will either double the size of your congregation in three years or double the amount of per capita giving across the board during that same period. In my view, such an ambitious goal is likely to stretch a congregation beyond its capabilities and create disappointment and discouragement rather than the desired result of participation and excitement about the project.

The key with any financial source or system is to choose your partners carefully. There are a number of top-notch firms across the country that promote and manage capital campaigns of this type. Most of them do an excellent job of training and leading a prayer focus that generates both the knowledge and the spiritual base for a successful campaign. Always check references and ask other pastors who have worked with a particular firm about their experiences. If the capital campaign approach fits the culture of your congregation, it can be extremely successful as long as the goal is set properly at the front end, the channels of communication are carefully established, and the members of your church are trained adequately to carry out their part of the plan.

Pay As You Go

Whether you can pay as you go on a substantial building project depends on how much cash flow you can generate and how quickly you think the construction can proceed. From what I've seen though, more often than not, pay-as-you-go projects that would normally take about eight to ten months of construction turn into five-, six-, or even seven-year marathons.

Efforts to pay as you go usually arise out of some aversion to debt, an inability to qualify for financing, or a desire to keep costs down by using volunteer labor. Unfortunately, the idea of using volunteer labor often goes hand in hand with a misplaced confidence in the congregation's ability to tackle a sizable construction project. I would advise any pastor or church leader, before tackling a project, to consider carefully whether the available volunteer base has the necessary skills.

Projects of this type often get off to a fast start, which gets everyone excited and involved, because the early stages—pouring the foundation and framing the walls—are relatively quick and easy to show progress. The difficulty starts after the building is up and closed in, because anyone who has ever worked with construction knows that once you get the rough structure done it takes forever by contrast to do the finish work. If you are doing it yourselves, the completion process can drive everybody batty. And, if you choose not to hire subcontractors—that is, people who will work on the project as part of their profession—and you are relying on volunteers to come in when they can, the process can drag on for a very long time.

Typically, a pay-as-you-go campaign will start with a couple of big work days when everybody comes out on a Saturday and bangs nails, saws wood, and accomplishes a good beginning. Those who like to paint are painting, those who like to cook are cooking, and those who enjoy carpentry are working on building various elements of the project. But at the end of the day, they all walk away and who shows up the next time? Usually it's the pastor and a few other individuals.

If the pastor isn't there with sawdust all over his ears, some people start to wonder, "Well, is he really committed?" And if he is there with sawdust all over his ears, other people wonder how much time he is able to spend on sermon preparation and shepherding the life of the church. Who makes the hospital calls while the pastor is on the job site swinging a hammer? Unfortunately, it doesn't take long to create a terrible tension within the congregation between the priorities of the building and the priorities of ministry, especially if the timeline starts to drag and people begin to get burned out. Prime candidates for burnout include the pastor, his wife and kids, and anybody else who is actively participating on a daily or weekly basis. The most typical line I've heard from pastors who have built on a pay-as-you-go basis is, "We built our church with volunteer labor, and I was the volunteer." It isn't that a pay-as-you-go approach can't work. But it can be very difficult and it depends a great deal on the scope of the project, the expertise of the workers, and the commitment of the congregation.

Quality of construction is another major concern with a pay-as-you-go approach because volunteer labor isn't necessarily qualified, skilled labor. Every time I hear a pastor say, "We'll just buy the materials and our guys will put the stuff up," I get a queasy feeling in my stomach. We have all seen buildings with walls that aren't quite plumb and joints that don't quite match. It seems obvious to say that you don't send a greenhorn in to route plumbing or pull wires, but believe me, it has been tried.

Using volunteer labor can work if you have a qualified supervisor who can train workers and oversee the process, but he needs to be an able communicator as well as a skilled worker. But if your best worker spends more time training the other volunteers than it would take to do the job himself, you're wasting a lot of time for no benefit.

Another word to the wise: Make sure that you have adequate insurance coverage on all volunteer workers. On the off chance that someone gets hurt, you can have real trouble if you're not covered. If you decide to use volunteer labor, you had better have workers' compensation coverage in force because a standard health care plan might not cover a work-related injury. And if an individual's health plan won't cover him, the church might be on the hook for his medical care and possible long-term disability. All it would take is one serious injury to wipe out any cost savings that might accrue from a pay-as-you-go approach.

Does a pay-as-you-go approach necessarily mean using volunteer labor? Certainly you will employ some subcontractors along the way who will be paid on a bid basis, but you are probably not going to contract the entire job because no contractor would take a job on which the customer calls him on Monday and says, "We need you this week, we had a good offering. But next week we aren't going to need you because we are going to be short of funds to keep the project moving." A contractor is not going to call on Monday morning and ask, "How was yesterday's offering? Shall I go to work, or not?" Scheduling, obviously, is a key part of an effective contractor's profitability.

Under a pay-as-you-go approach, you will probably call in an electrician or a plumber for a specific part of the job, but scheduling is often a challenge because certain functions must be completed before other parts of the job can start. For example, all of the wires must be in the walls before you can put up the Sheetrock. Of course, you first need to have the money and labor to install the wiring. Everything is dependent on something else. Let's say that to do your pay-as-you-go project, you arrange for some individuals in your church to pull wires and you are trying to schedule a subcontractor to come in and do the Sheetrock work. What happens if the volunteers don't get all of the wires run in time for the Sheetrock workers? If your subcontractor shows up with his full work crew, he is going to take one look at the job, say, "This isn't ready," and walk off the building site. Ask yourself how easy it is going to be to get that subcontractor back. Meanwhile, you have your Sheetrock lying around outside, and if it starts raining, the problems begin to mount.

These issues can seem insignificant individually, but as they begin to accumulate, they can become monumental. Scheduling can be a very expensive issue in a construction project. One of the reasons that we have professional building contractors is because scheduling is a "value-added" function, and part of a builder's expertise is getting things done right and on time.

Another way in which delays can drive up the cost of construction is if your subcontractor gets busy on other jobs while he is waiting for you to get your act together. What happens to prices when demand goes up? All of a sudden, the bid that you based your budget on is no longer valid. When you call your subcontractor, he says, "Hey, we're real busy right now and I can no longer do the job at that price because I would have to pull my guys off other jobs."

Far too many churches have had disastrous pay-as-you-go building projects for such reasons. It is difficult enough to keep the vision alive, but try to do it when the building process takes from three to five years instead of eight to ten months. And how many changes get worked into the plan along the way? Do those changes affect the traffic flow into the building? Do they affect fire code and other issues that may become stumbling blocks when you try to get your occupancy permit? There's something to be said for momentum, flow, and progress on a building project.

In my view, pay as you go makes sense only if your project is relatively small and you can get it done quickly with volunteer labor and maybe one or two subcontractors. If the project is any more complex than that, wisdom would dictate that you find another way to get it done. Otherwise, I believe that you will end up overtaxing your congregation and delaying the project. Frankly, I'm not sure that you will end up saving as much as you think you will because problems with scheduling will tend to push up the price.

Borrowing from an Outside Source

The case for borrowing is, among other things, one of speed and convenience. Generally speaking, you can get your project rolling more quickly when you borrow the necessary resources. If it is also easily affordable, then it might also make sense from that standpoint, depending on how it fits into your philosophy of debt.

If you decide to borrow, commercial banks are certainly a viable option. In fact, they are the single largest provider of capital financing for churches across the country. Denominational resources, for their part, tend to be a bit more flexible and frequently are somewhat more economical in terms of closing costs and fees. I say they *tend* to be this way because it is not true in all circumstances.

Each lender will have specific rules of thumb for determining how much you can borrow, including ratios of loan value to security value, the percentage of your regular cash flow that can be used for debt service, and other underwriting issues. Generally speaking, most lenders will loan between 50 percent and 80 percent of the finished value of the property and building. Often, they will allow between 25 percent and 33 percent of the general fund of the church to be used for debt service. Using these two factors, you can calculate with reasonable certainty the borrowing limitations that your church may face.

Note that church bond lenders, who may go as high as 80 percent on their loan-to-value ratios, may still be in the 25 percent to 30 percent range with respect to general fund cash flow because they are primarily cash-flow lenders. Every lender will look at your church's track record of revenue and expenses to determine whether the general operations of the church will support the projected level of financial obligation. Cash-flow lenders, such as most bond underwriters, tend to spend a lot of time looking at the composition of your general fund revenues to establish if they are a fairly reliable resource.

Most lenders will concern themselves with the church budget and whether ample income exists to support repayment of the loan. Generally, they will want to establish that the church's overall ministry can continue unencumbered and that the church won't become simply a debt-servicing organization.

Commercial Banks

In most situations, borrowing from a commercial bank is a straightforward transaction, much like borrowing for a mortgage on a house. Note, however, that the terms and conditions of financing a church building are substantially different than a straight residential loan. As soon as you approach a bank for a church loan, you are talking about a commercial transaction, which will have a rate structure and terms different than a typical home loan. Be aware that the church will not be able to secure a thirty-year, fixed-rate loan like you would expect on a home mortgage. Instead, it is far more likely that your interest rate will be adjusted periodically through the term of the loan, and you will have a fifteen- or twenty-year amortization schedule but with a balloon payment due in seven to ten years. Such terms are fairly standard in commercial capital financing.

Another customary element of commercial financing is "personal guarantees," which I would recommend you avoid at all costs. It is not uncommon for a bank to ask a church to have some of its members sign the note as additional guarantors on a joint-and-several basis. What this means legally is that each guarantor is on the hook for the full amount of the loan if the church defaults. Personal guarantees are a bad deal for several reasons.

If you think about it for a moment, you'll no doubt realize that only those members who are strongly committed to the church would even consider making such a guarantee. And yet, as soon as they put their own credit rating on the line in the form of a guarantee, their relationship with the church changes. Emotionally, they may feel as though they are now part of leadership, even if they are not already on your church board. Personal guarantees inevitably change the relationship between the pastor and the guarantor and can produce some very interesting and difficult interpersonal dynamics.

Another factor that must be understood with personal guarantees is that the bank will record the guarantee, making it a matter of public record. This means that the next time a credit report is released for the individuals who signed the guarantee, it will show that they are guarantors of not just a portion of the church loan but of the entire loan.

This situation actually happened. A member of a church about which I heard had a net worth of just over $1 million, including his house and a few investments. He signed a $500,000 joint-and-several guarantee on behalf of his church and thought nothing of it. Later that year, when he went out to buy his daughter a used car to take to college, he was turned down for the loan because his credit report showed a $500,000 obligation in a joint-and-several guarantee. He was understandably upset and came back to express his concerns to the pastor.

The moral of the story is that if you are asked to sign a personal guarantee on behalf of the church, first consider all of the ramifications and go in with your eyes wide open. My advice, however, to both leaders in the church and individuals, is to avoid personal guarantees whenever possible.

Denominational Sources

Many denominations and fellowships have organizations that make loans to churches and ministries for capital improvements. Quite often these entities are combination lending and investing firms in which members and friends of the denomination can invest reserve funds or retirement savings, which in turn are loaned out to churches and ministries. My company, Church Extension Plan, is this type of organization, providing conservative investment opportunities for members and friends of our denomination and loaning funds for building and improving church facilities for congregations in the denomination.

Denominational sources are often more flexible than commercial companies because of the lender's ties of brotherhood and ministry with the churches and ministries requiring financial assistance. Frequently, their rates are at or below those of commercial sources, and their fees are quite often lower than those of a commercial bank or other resource. Some denominational sources operate in a manner similar to commercial lenders but with more of a focus on ministry. This is decidedly different than the stance of most commercial lenders. Still, it is important to remember that even denominational programs will have—and should have—clear standards for underwriting a loan. Regardless of the source of funds, rates, ratios, terms, and conditions are all a normal part of the business and should be expected.

Bond Programs

Compared to more traditional methods of borrowing, bond programs can be more expensive in terms of related fees, and they might be relatively complex to establish, but many churches believe that a bond program gives them more control and flexibility than they would have with a traditional bank loan or financing through a denominational source.

A church can issue a bond in several ways. One approach would be to retain an attorney who would develop a bond offering using the forms and approaches approved by your state's security regulatory agencies. More often than not, however, a church will seek the advice and assistance of a professional bond consultant or underwriter.

Construction bonds fall into one of four categories, depending on how they are underwritten or funded and how they are secured. The two ways in which a bond can be funded are called "firm underwriting" and "best efforts."

With firm underwriting, the investment banking organization that is developing the bond will commit to make available a certain amount of money on a certain date to fund the construction needs of the church. The underwriter will then sell the bonds, either within the congregation that is issuing the bond, or through other established markets across the country. The key here is that the bond underwriter takes full responsibility for selling the bonds and guarantees to the church that the funds will be available on a particular date.

With a best-efforts program, the underwriters use their "best efforts" to sell the entire bond package to members and friends of the church that is seeking the financing. As individuals purchase shares of the bond, their funds are deposited into an escrow account until the entire bond has been sold. If the program does not sell out within the congregation, the underwriters have one of two options. They can either return any committed funds to the original investors and close out the program, or they can sell the bonds in other markets to complete the funding.

As you would expect, firm-underwriting and best-effort programs have different fee structures and qualification standards, and their own advantages and disadvantages. Firm underwriting programs tend to be somewhat more expensive than best efforts because the underwriter is assuming a greater risk, but if your church qualifies, you will get faster funding and a guaranteed sale of the bonds in exchange for those higher fees. In essence, a "firm" underwriter is certifying that on a specific date they will deposit the full amount of your bond offering into your account. They will market those bonds within your congregation, if you approve that approach, and in other markets as necessary. Alternatively, a best-efforts program will be slightly less expensive, but a real possibility exists that the bonds might not be fully sold within your congregation. Usually, additional fees will be charged if the underwriter has to sell into other sectors of the market, or the bond program will simply be deemed not fully funded and the amount already invested will be returned, in which case the church must start over with a different financing option.

Bonds may also differ by how they are secured, either through mortgage or debenture. A mortgage bond is one whereby the underlying real estate is pledged as collateral for the bond offering, so that the individuals who purchase shares have ultimate security in the value of the church property. A debenture bond, on the other hand, is technically an unsecured bond that is issued based on the revenue flow or credit rating of the congregation and not on the lien value of the real estate. Rate structures will vary based on the current market conditions when the bond is issued.

Covering the "Swing Point"

All of the capital financing programs that I have described share a common potential for difficulty, a place that I call the "swing point," where many churches miscalculate their cash requirements. The swing point is that period of time when you are beginning to make payments on the money you've borrowed to start your building project, yet you are still renting or making payments on your old building. Even assuming that you have set up a progressive funding plan whereby you borrow additional increments of money only as you need them during the nine or ten months of construction, your outstanding obligation and corresponding payment will begin to ramp up as the building nears completion. If you haven't allowed for the double payment (the new loan and the old rent), you can find yourself in a sudden cash-flow crisis. My advice is always to try to take nine or ten months' worth of payments, and generate a reserve fund out of general fund surpluses or building fund gifts so that you can cover the swing point out of cash reserves rather than trying to manage two payments out of your operating budget.

If your church does not have the necessary cash flow to cover the swing point, you may need to negotiate with the lender to defer payments and put them on the back end of the loan—in essence, negatively amortizing for a short period of time. Certainly, that is not the best circumstance in which to be because it can be more expensive in terms of interest expense, but it's one way to get yourselves over the hump. If you do negatively amortize at the beginning of your loan, I strongly suggest that you attempt to accelerate payments for a set period of time early in the life of your loan so that you don't end up paying excess interest by extending the term of the loan beyond what you originally planned.

Because determining the best type of financing for your church depends so heavily on your specific circumstances, attempting more than a general overview of the various alternatives would quickly grow beyond the scope of this book. The keys to a successful experience, however, are the same for every congregation: Do your homework, explore and compare your options, and bathe the entire process in prayer before you settle on a course of action. Ensure that the financing option you select meshes well with your church's culture and your understanding of financial stewardship.

Chapter 6

ESTABLISHING YOUR BUILDING COMMITTEE

EARLY IN THE PLANNING process, you should select a building committee—a group of trusted, committed, active members, who represent the various ministries of the church—who will help the pastor and the board preside over the building process. The members of the building committee likely will be drawn from other existing groups within the church, including people who have already assisted in the casting of the church's vision, ministry planning, and implementation. Often, they will be key volunteers who head areas of ministry within the church and, therefore, have specific knowledge of the needs of each area.

I would suggest that you limit your core committee to no more than five or six people and that each member represent larger subcommittees organized around specific ministry needs. In an average-size church, the core committee would probably consist of the pastor, the board chairman, the communications subcommittee chairman, the finance subcommittee chairman, the construction subcommittee chairman, the ministry subcommittee chairman, and the prayer subcommittee chairman.

If you want your building plans to reflect accurately the congregation's needs, wants, and dreams, it's important that the building committee include a representative from every key ministry group within the church. In other words, you don't want to design classroom space without first getting input from the leaders of your Sunday school, or child-care space without participation from your nursery coordinator. The same principle applies across the spectrum. The more representative of the full range of ministries in the church your committee is, the more balanced and comprehensive your building plan will be and the easier it will be to build consensus within the congregation.

The senior pastor may serve as a key liaison to the staff of the church, but he should avoid, if at all possible, chairing the building committee. He should try to remain somewhat "above the fray," ready to speak to issues of vision, spiritual matters, and conflict resolution without becoming overly involved in details that might distract from his main responsibilities of shepherding and teaching.

The chairman of the board may serve as the key liaison to the rest of the board, but he also should avoid chairing the building committee unless another suitable leader fails to emerge.

Building Committee Responsibilities

Initially, the building committee's job will be to review the ministry plan, determine appropriate timelines, and set parameters on the master-planning effort. They will be closely involved in interviewing architects and builders and will make recommendations to the full board or congregation for their consideration. The core group will also keep a close eye on the budget. As the building plan begins to take shape, the committee is responsible for maintaining consistency and compliance with the church's mission and vision statements. At each stage of the process, committee members will be responsible for building consensus throughout the congregation and helping the pastor communicate the plan effectively.

The members of the building committee will also oversee

subcommittees that will focus on specific areas of ministry or specialized aspects of the building process. The number and range of subcommittees will vary, based on the size of your church, but at a minimum, you will want to create groups to focus on the following areas.

- *Prayer.* Gather a team of committed intercessors to pray for every step of the process. The chairman of the prayer committee will be responsible for conveying key issues and concerns to the group, who can pray consistently, specifically, and intentionally throughout the project. In my view, it is essential that this group be given specific representation on the building committee so that it is clear to everyone that prayer is an integral part of the plan and not an afterthought. Accordingly, this group should be active right from the start.
- *Finance.* One of the first responsibilities of the building committee is to establish a budget. The more precise you can be in your communication with your architect, planner, and contractor, the better your chances of ending up with the building you want at a price you can afford. Without good financial information and oversight, you're really shooting in the dark, and you can spend an awful lot of money doing and redoing elements of the building plan that should have to be done only once.

  The finance subcommittee will be responsible to assist the staff and the board with the evaluation and execution of the financial plan for the project, including the selection of financing options, the evaluation of budgets and bids, etc. Obviously, the person selected to chair this committee should possess the necessary skills and financial expertise to provide wise leadership and counsel.
- *Ministry.* The ministry subcommittee is responsible for collaborating with the staff and key volunteers of the congregation to articulate clearly the ministries of the church in a way that the architect can use to develop

space plans. Every key ministry within the church should have representation on this important subcommittee.

- *Communication.* This group is absolutely essential for disseminating important information to the rest of the congregation in a timely fashion. The communications subcommittee will ensure that the congregation and other constituencies of the church are kept informed of the progress of the project. This subcommittee is a good place for key opinion leaders, writers, and artists to participate in the building project. You may include members who were instrumental in developing and communicating the church's mission and vision statements because the building project is an extension of the overall vision. Of course, communication of the overall vision should be completed well before a new building begins to take shape, but the communication process extends all of the way through the dedication of the new facility.
- *Construction.* This subcommittee should include one or more experts with experience in the building trades who can oversee the construction process to ensure that everything is proceeding according to plan. If you don't have any qualified contractors in your congregation, you would be well advised to hire a neutral third party who can stop by the job site regularly to evaluate the progress and report back to the subcommittee. Ensure that the contractors you select for the oversight committee don't have a conflict of interest (or a bone to pick) with the contractor hired to do the construction.

  The construction subcommittee should comprise a small group of individuals with specific construction experience who can work with the building committee to evaluate the progress of the project. Their key contributions will include evaluating plans and bids and overseeing implementation of the construction. The chairman of this committee will be responsible for a periodic walk-through of the project and regular progress reports to the building committee.

Subcommittee Responsibilities

The main purpose of the subcommittees is research and development. Each subcommittee will have a specific area of focus. Their job is to generate ideas; find out what's available, what works, and what doesn't work; research various options and costs; and begin to narrow a list of needs, wants, and desires for their area of interest. They should go out and look at other churches and talk to other people to get ideas for things they want to recommend to the building committee.

Subcommittees are an excellent way to broaden the involvement of the congregation, attract gifted individuals, and focus on the needs of specific ministries without overloading the main planning committee with too many voices. Only the chairman of each subcommittee would be a member of the core building committee.

The number and size of your subcommittees depends on the size of your church and the size of the project. In a smaller church, both these subcommittees and the main building committee will be small. Everything will be according to scale. Depending on the size of your church, your list of subcommittees may include some or all of the following:

- Christian education/Sunday school
- Youth (junior high, high school, and college)
- Nursery/toddlers/child care
- Site selection
- Interior design/furniture/decoration
- Music/worship
- Sanctuary
- Sound and lights
- Drama
- Landscaping

- Parking
- Christian school
- Senior care
- Food closet/outreach to the poor
- Food service/kitchen/fellowship space
- Building maintenance
- Office and administrative staff
- Counseling ministries
- Sports and recreation

Once your building committee and subcommittees have been selected, don't hesitate to put them to work. Done properly, the job will take a significant amount of time. For example, your music subcommittee might want to start by defining the musical personality of the church. Is it orchestral? Choral music? Musical programs? Is your worship accompanied by a piano and organ, a single guitar player, or a full band? What are the acoustical requirements for the sanctuary to match your style of worship? Subcommittee members might visit a number of churches of comparable size in the area to see how they accommodate their musicians and choirs, how they store their instruments securely so they aren't damaged or stolen, what they've learned about acoustics and sound systems—whatever list of questions your subcommittee can devise to study every aspect of music in the church. Meanwhile, all of the other subcommittees will be conducting similar studies for their areas of concern.

When the reports come back from the various subcommittees, the building committee will review the suggested options, assess the church's needs, and establish a list of priorities. What you will end up with is a ton of ideas, probably only one-third of which you can afford, but at least you can begin to prioritize them. These priorities then pour into the master plan, so that when you go to your architect you can say, "We're really big on music in our church, and these are the kinds of facilities we need. We also have a thriving nursery and toddler ministry, and here's what we need to accommodate those people." The more specific information you can provide to your architect, the easier it will be for him to draw plans that will meet your needs.

At our church in California, the "must have" list from our nursery subcommittee included the following items:

- minimum square footage requirements,
- location close to the sanctuary,
- capability to communicate with the sanctuary,
- surfaces that are easy to keep clean and sanitary,
- a sink, and
- provision for cleaning up spills.

We ended up not being able to do everything that the subcommittee wanted in terms of design, but we had all of the essential requirements (needs) and many of their wants and dreams.

Pulling It All Together

After each subcommittee has submitted its proposal or made its presentation, the building committee must do the hard work of sorting all of the needs, wants, and dreams into a master list of priorities—always with an eye toward balancing the vision with the budget and keeping the overall ministry of the church in perspective. List your priorities in descending order, with the understanding that, although every item is important, some items are more important than others and some of the lower-priority items may get bumped from the list as you go along.

This comprehensive priority list then becomes an essential part of the communication document that the building committee will give to the architect or planner. Working through all of this information is not easy, but it is absolutely essential if you want to end up with the best building at the best possible price. Where it gets sticky is when the architect comes back and says, "Based on the budget you've given me, you can't afford to do what you've proposed. We can't even satisfy your minimum requirements, let alone your wants and dreams." Then what are you going to do?

If your initial plan is too ambitious, the first corrective step is to find out how far over budget the basic plan is. Can you make up the difference with additional fundraising? You might need to shrink the scope of your project, divide it into phases, make some of the spaces smaller or more efficient, or eliminate some things entirely. These are some of the hard decisions that your building committee might need to make in collaboration with your architect. The most difficult spot is when you can't afford even your bare minimum expectations and you really have to roll your project back. That might mean going back to your subcommittees and asking them to review their recommendations and decide what can be pulled out of the plan to fit within the budget. Usually the answer is, "Nothing. We can't pull out anything."

"OK, but if you have to pull something out, what's it going to be?"

Even if the architect comes back with the good news that most of your wants and dreams are affordable, the committee will want to review the items that were dropped to see if any last-minute trade-offs are necessary to keep everyone happy.

The Communication Document

When the building committee has completed all of the preliminary work, it's time to publish a communication document to convey essential information to the architect or planner in a simple, easy-to-read format. At the very least, this document should include the following information:

- budget;
- master list of priorities (needs, wants, and dreams); and
- site information (if known), including lot size, access

information, plat map, topographical map, and soil compositions report.

This document becomes the primary communication tool to transmit all the necessary information to the planner or architect so that he or she can begin to design your facility.

Also, once you have the report of your planning committee, along with a keen view of your financial capability, it's time to communicate with your church membership. Ultimately, you will need the church's direction either for action on remodeling, relocating, or acquiring properties or the go-ahead for a master plan, depending on which phase of development you're in. To vote appropriately on the future plans for the church, your congregation must be fully informed.

Chapter 7

THE MASTER PLAN

ONCE THE VISION-CASTING process has been completed and your building committee has done its job of identifying your needs, wants, and desires for ministry space and facilities, you can look at your current physical structure and determine whether it's going to be sufficient. Depending on how ambitious your vision statement is, you should have a pretty good idea about whether you will need to build a new facility, add to your existing building, or simply remodel or renovate your current space.

If some form of expansion is needed, now would be a good time to hire a master planner to talk through the vision and begin to map out how many square feet you're going to need and how it might fit with your current facility. If you have enough room on your current property for both the new buildings and any additional parking that might be required, the planner can develop some schematic drawings of how your enlarged facility might look, how the buildings will lay out on your lot, and how they can be integrated into your current facility.

Master planning is a vital part of the overall building process, even if you are only adding on to an existing structure. It would be helpful to have a long-term plan that can project your needs five or ten years into the future to determine what can or cannot be accomplished on your current site. If it turns out that you're going to have to relocate, the planner can help you determine how much property you will need to acquire to accomplish the objectives spelled out in your vision statement. Even if you don't plan to move right away, it isn't too early to begin scouting the neighborhood or community for suitable locations. The size of the property you need might dictate where you can look, and the sooner you start the search process, the more time you'll have to work through any zoning issues, contingencies, or delays. We'll talk more about site selection later, but for now suffice it to say that it's never too soon to start looking.

How to Know When It's Time to Build

How far in advance should you start thinking about building? It depends on the magnitude of the project, of course, but it's usually wise to start looking ahead. I can't imagine myself pastoring a church where I wouldn't be trying to identify the trigger points that would tell us that it's time to build. Is it going to be Sunday morning attendance or overflow in the nursery or the parking lot? Where are we pushing the seams? And then, what are we going to need? What needs in the body or in the community will we have to satisfy first? I think that every pastor ought to be thinking about such issues.

In a perfect world, we would carefully plan our work and deliberately work our plans, and everything would go along smoothly. In the real world, however, it usually takes a motivating circumstance—a positive opportunity or negative pressure—to stimulate us to action. The same principle applies to church construction. Even if we have a well-articulated vision statement, it often takes a jolt to move us along our timeline. Are you being pushed toward the inevitable conclusion that you need more space by an exploding nursery, traffic jams in the parking lot, or the prospect of adding a third service (all good problems, I suppose, if you have to have a problem), or are you being drawn forward by the passionate pursuit of God's vision for your church? If your vision is forward-looking, energizing, and ambitious, it really will propel the decision. You can look ahead and say, "If the Lord blesses us and we stay on target, by such and such a date we should be at a certain level of attendance, a certain level of Sunday school, a certain level of cell group involvement," or whatever the trigger points might be.

Generally speaking, you know it's time to build when it becomes too painful not to. How quickly a project moves along is proportional to the amount of pain the congregation is feeling. If you're desperate, if the neighbors are threatening to start towing cars, or if the fire marshal has issued a warning, the process can accelerate rapidly. If the pressure is self-manufactured by forward-looking leaders who realize "If we don't get going on our project, by the time we get to our trigger point, we're going to be hamstrung by our building," the building project can proceed at a more intentional and deliberate pace.

Engaging a Master Planner

When you hit one of your trigger points, will you be ready to move forward? You will if you've already done some planning. If you know you're going to have to expand or relocate, it probably makes sense to pay an architect to sit down now and review your vision and come up with a master plan. Based on your vision statement, you ought to be able to tell the planner, "Here's what we're absolutely going to need, here are some things we want to have, and here are some 'dream' items that we'd love to have if there's enough money." Have the architect work from the top down until he hits the limits of your budget. That way you get the maximum out of what you can afford. Getting a plan that meets your needs and maximizes your budget justifies the decision to spend the money today for a plan that you might not build for three, four, or five years. The plan might change and therefore need to be tweaked as you go along, but at least you have a firm basis on which to proceed.

I strongly recommend that you spend the necessary dollars

(usually $2000–$4000) to develop a master plan. Ask the architect or planner to lay out a footprint for the building or buildings that you expect to need in the long run. Be certain to take into account set-back requirements and other restrictions that the city or county might impose.

The Master Planning Timetable

How long does it take to devise a master plan? If you have done your homework; have a well-crafted document from your planning committee that articulates your needs, wants, and dreams; can communicate the worship atmosphere and all of the other pieces that give the architect some sense of spatial issues; have a plat map that shows the boundaries of your property; know the location of your utilities; and have a topographical map that shows the lay of the land, it should take only as long as it takes the planner or architect to conceptualize and draw the design—probably no more than a month. One month is a reasonable expectation—if you've done your homework.

A completed master plan is a drawing that depicts the layout of the land, traffic ingress and egress, and at least a schematic representation of where the buildings will sit, starting with the first phase. Phase one is usually drawn with hard lines, and subsequent phases are drawn as dotted or shadowed lines so that it's apparent that they are not part of the immediate plan. Once you have your master plan and have determined your course of action, it will be helpful to develop color renderings or other models to be used as part of your vision-sharing and fund-raising efforts.

You don't need fine detail to initiate an overview plan, but as soon as you try to impose any kind of structure onto those squares and rectangles, you'd better have all of the details worked out. Otherwise, you're going to be redrawing your plans, and that is going to get expensive. For example, you need to think through whether you plan to have ball fields or other outside play areas or classroom space and a gymnasium for a school.

All of those issues will dictate how much land you need and how your buildings will lay out.

Form follows function. You must be able to articulate the human side of your vision and how your ministry is going to look. What are people going to be doing and where? Are these people going to be infants, toddlers, teens, adults, families, or singles? Will they be rowdy or quiet? If you have a noisy group in one room, what's going to be happening next door? How will people get from one part of the facility to another—singly or in groups? Will it be rainy, sunny, or snowy? All of these factors affect the thinking of a designer.

In some parts of the country, you can have an open patio between buildings with no problem. In the Pacific Northwest, you need a covered breezeway to keep off the rain. In the Northeast, you must enclose the passageways or winter snows will blow in. In a lot of California churches, you can open the front door and walk directly into the foyer. In most other areas, you open the front door and walk into a windlock, then open another door and go into the foyer. Southeastern churches all have windlocks because it's also a barrier to keep in the air-conditioning. In California, open patios are used as fellowship areas because people want to get outside after the service. In rainy Oregon, however, open patios don't work very well for most of the year.

Traffic patterns are another important consideration. In one church I've seen, the congregation enters through one set of doors and exits through another because there isn't enough room in the foyer for two-way traffic. The side exit doors lead directly to the parking lot, with no breezeway or fellowship area. Once you're out, you're on your way.

Master Planning Before Site Acquisition

Ideally, a master plan will be drawn for an existing site, but you might need to go through some level of master planning even before you acquire land to ensure that you purchase a plot large enough to do the things you intend to do. On the other hand, the topography and other features of a particular plot will determine its suitability, usability, and situation of the facility, so determining the proper time to initiate a master plan is a balancing act to some degree. But if you've been diligent to articulate your vision and have at least preliminary numbers on a budget, you can begin to define the parameters that will govern your site-selection process.

Do you need three, ten, or twenty-five acres? Before you engage the services of an architect or planner, you at least want to be far enough along with your vision development that you are able to say, "Here's how we foresee our needs," and have the architect give you a rule of thumb for space requirements. He might say, "You'll need five acres for the building, three acres for parking, and six acres for ball fields, setbacks, and landscaping—which adds up to fourteen acres, so you'd better be looking for at least a fourteen-acre site."

If you end up with a large variance between what you think you might need on the low end and the maximum you'll need on the high end (say a range from five to fifteen acres), I strongly recommend that you commission a master plan and tell the planner that you need not only suggested placement of buildings on a relatively flat piece of land but also some concept of the minimum acreage necessary to accommodate the plan and recommendations for upside leeway. If he estimates that you could "get by" with eight acres, ask, "How tight will that be?" Would you be better off with ten acres—or twelve? Optimum land requirements, building size and layout, setbacks and other zoning restrictions—these are the kinds of issues about which you need to talk with your planner. It would be foolhardy to say, "We need twenty acres"—or two acres—without having in place an overall concept and plan.

Reviewing the Plan

Ultimately, your plan has to work within your budget. Obviously, the cost of the land will be a major component of the overall project expense, but this is not just a two-axis decision. Planning is multi-dimensional; every decision pushes something else.

One thing you can do to keep your costs in line is to avoid change orders by investing the time to review the initial plans very carefully. When you get the preliminary drawings from the architect, mentally walk through each space and ask, "Are the rooms logically arranged? Are the bathrooms where they should be? Does the child care space seem adequate? Is this going to be a dark corner? Does this area need a window? What would happen if we had a door here? Would it improve access? How easy will it be for a visitor to find his way around?"

Many of us don't have experience visualizing from plans to finished look, so you need to find some people on your committee who can do that. Do your best and be as thorough as you can be. If you can't visualize it, at least talk it through. "OK, I'm walking through this door. Is it clear how I get to the sanctuary from here?" Mentally walk through the whole building and ask as many questions as you can because, at this early stage, changes are relatively inexpensive. Encourage your committee to bring up all of their thoughts, questions, and recommendations; they must not hold back at this stage. The last thing you want is for someone to walk into the finished building and say, "I knew it was going to look like this"—or worse, "I was afraid it was going to look like this." Get all of those premonitions, fears, ideas, and questions out on the table before the final plans are drawn and certainly before construction commences. Anything that can be done to avoid change orders is going to be time efficient and cost effective.

Have several people—not just your experts—look at the plans. Some of the best questions come from people who don't necessarily know how to read plans but who can visualize what things ought to look like and can articulate questions that need to be asked. Talk through the plans thoroughly with your building committee, and don't shut down the discussion until everyone has been encouraged to interact with the plans and ask all of their questions. Again, the earlier you make your changes, the less it will cost.

Of course, if you want to avoid the cost of changing plans altogether, the time really to think through what you want is in the vision and planning stages. The more information you can give to your architect up front, the better the plans you will get back. But whatever you do, don't skip over or hurry through the "plan evaluation" stage.

Don't allow the architect or the builder to rush you through the approval process. In fact, they should be walking through the plans with you and helping you to articulate questions and anticipate concerns. Time spent up front is always worth it down the road. The adage "An ounce of prevention is worth a pound of cure" is unquestionably true when it comes to blueprints and buildings.

Representatives from each constituent group within the church should look at the composite plan, but they must especially scrutinize those areas that apply directly to them to ensure that everything they need is included. A careful review of the plans by the people who will be living most closely with the outcome can avoid 75 percent of your change orders.

Establishing Good Working Relationships

There is no substitute for good communication with your architect and your builder. You want these folks on your side, working with you and helping you to avoid pitfalls. Be direct and thorough. Finish each conversation with your architect and builder by asking, "Are there any questions that we're not asking that we *should* be asking?" Don't be afraid to explore specific details of the plan, especially where the planner may have specified something that might be more or less than what you need and where you might want to make an informed decision about what you really want.

For example, one church of which I'm aware decided to change the doorknobs they had originally specified. The new doorknobs were safer and more substantial, with a longer deadbolt, and cost only $2 apiece more than the old ones. However, unbeknownst to the building committee, the installation process was substantially different, requiring a significant increase in labor. Because the committee was unaware of the differences—because they thought that a doorknob was just a doorknob—and they didn't bother to check, their labor costs for installation skyrocketed.

The committee should have asked the right questions, but a contractor who was thinking on his feet and communicating well with his customer would have said, "Hold on. This looks like a simple switch of doorknobs, but the installation process for this second one is 50 percent more time-consuming. And when you multiply that by twenty-five doorknobs, it becomes a fairly substantial change. Is that really what you want to do?" In the long run, the new doorknob was probably a good choice, but it affected the budget, and the church would have preferred to have made an informed decision.

I cannot overemphasize the importance of careful and complete communication at each stage of the building process. When we were building our church in California, for example, our contractor came to us one day and said, "Do you really want the light fixtures that the architect specified?"

I said, "I don't know. Why wouldn't we?"

"Well, you said that you're going to have a flexible office system, with partitions that could potentially be moved around. The architect interpreted that to mean that you need maximum flexibility in your lighting system, and he specified a system where we run conduit above the T-bar ceiling, such that you can literally unplug a light fixture, pull it down, move it over one bay and plug it back in. You have unlimited flexibility with your lights, but it costs $45,000 more than a hard-wired light."

I asked, "For $45,000, how many electricians can we hire to move lights if we need to?"

The builder replied, "My point exactly."

We calculated that hiring an electrician to reposition a light fixture, including any rewiring and additional junction boxes, might cost $150. At that rate, how many times would we have to change the lights before we'd spend $45,000? The decision was simple: we authorized the change to hard-wired fixtures.

The point is self-evident: you must communicate carefully. Obviously, the architect didn't understand what we meant by "flexibility." He interpreted it through his own grid, and he didn't ask questions to clarify our needs and expectations. He should have explained to us, during the walk-through of the plans, that he had specified a particular light fixture, which offered maximum flexibility but that it was more costly than other options. We then would have had the opportunity to ask, "How much more costly?" Then, if he had said, "About $45,000," we would have replied, "Let's not do that."

Ensure that your architect specifies fixtures and features that are suitable for the level of use they will receive. Suitability cuts both ways. You don't want a lesser grade of carpet, for example, in a high-traffic area, but neither do you want top-of-the-line materials in low-traffic areas.

On another church project, the architect specified bathroom fixtures like you would find in an airport bathroom, suitable for thousands of uses per day year round. At the time, the church had a staff of twenty-five. They didn't need high-end fixtures—or the additional expense.

When you communicate your needs, wants, and desires to your architect and building contractor, make very clear that you want to do everything possible to save costs while still building a structure that is serviceable, representative, and economical. Ask a lot of questions, and if you don't understand their response or if something seems a bit odd, ask for clarification. Remember, the building will be with you for many years, and it can be either a blessing or an albatross. Careful planning and clear communication are essential for achieving positive results.

Chapter 8

SITE SELECTION

I CAN'T COUNT THE number of times I've heard pastors say, "We're going to buy three acres and build a new building for our church." Whenever I hear such a statement, I always ask, "How do you know that three acres is enough?"

Inevitably, the pastor will shrug, and then I ask my second question: "Do you have your mission statement and your vision statement in place, and have you formed a building committee to research your needs, wants, and desires so that you know what kind of facility you need to build and how much land you need to build it?" More often than not, they don't and they haven't.

If you're moving ahead with a building project but you haven't taken the time to clarify your mission and articulate your vision for the future of your congregation, you're jumping the gun and courting great difficulty—if not disaster. Constructing a church building doesn't involve rocket science, although the potential for misfires and explosive mistakes might suggest otherwise, but it does require more than a good set of blueprints and a level piece of ground.

One church with which I worked was planning to purchase three acres of a larger parcel that was for sale. When we sat down to talk about the direction of their ministry and began unwrapping their vision, all of a sudden they were talking about building a grade school here and a high school there and several other buildings as well. I immediately stopped the conversation and said, "Time out! How are you going to put all of that on three acres?"

They had no idea.

After calculating their needs based on their vision for the future, they ended up buying seventeen acres, which allowed them eventually to achieve their long-term goals. Without a clearly articulated vision, however, they wouldn't have accurately anticipated their needs, they would have under bought their land—even though sufficient acreage was available—and it would have limited the expansion of their ministry. That's why starting with your mission and your vision is so important.

Grounding Your Search in Prayer

Even more basic than your mission and vision statements in the site-selection process is the necessity of prayer. It sounds almost too obvious to say it, but always start with prayer. Don't gloss over it and don't stop praying until you see the Lord answer. Ask Him to show you where to look and to show you the specific site that He has in mind for your congregation. Pray, "We want to do Your will, Lord, on Your site—not the one with which we're going to fall in love, but the one that You have for us."

It is so easy to forget to ask God, "What do You want to do here? What's Your vision for our church, for our ministry?" We can get so busy "doing God's work" that we forget to talk to Him about it. If you are seeking the will of the Lord and you have prayed through and developed a vision statement, is there even the remotest chance that God won't tell you where your building site should be?

As you persist in prayer, enlist the help of a real estate agent to get an idea of where the market is, and begin looking at property. Find out the average cost of a buildable acre. In 1979, when we were looking for property for our church in Dublin, California, the cost of a buildable acre on the San Ramon Valley floor was $50,000, plus utilities. That was beyond our financial capacity. We knew that we needed at least ten acres, probably fifteen, and within the confines of our ten-year plan, there was no way that we could spend $50,000 per acre and still do what we hoped to do with the building.

At first, we became discouraged, but then we said, "Well, God has a plan." While we continued to pray and waited for the Lord to reveal His purposes, we did all of the normal and natural things. We walked sites with several real estate agents. We drove around looking for possible locations and rang doorbells to see if the owners were willing to sell. We did *everything*, but we still didn't find a suitable location.

One day, I was sitting in my office at the church when a man wearing bib overalls walked in and said, "I understand you're looking for land."

"Yep," I replied, giving him the once-over.

"I've got some property you need to look at."

At first, I was skeptical because I thought we had already seen all of the available acreage in the area. I said, "We've looked at all of the land. Where is it?"

"I know you haven't looked at this land," he continued without missing a beat. "Do you want to go for a ride?"

"Sure," I shrugged.

We drove out to the edge of the valley and then hiked up a hill to a parcel that looked out over the entire area. It was absolutely gorgeous, with a fabulous, long-range view, and it was clearly visible from the valley floor up. I was intrigued, but my immediate thought was, *How much is this going to cost?*

The man started telling me about the property. He said, "Yeah, there's forty-nine acres here . . ."

Forty-nine acres! What in the world do we need with forty-nine acres?

". . . and I want $115,000 for it."

"Per acre?" I gulped.

"No, total," he said. "Twenty-five hundred per acre."

I wanted to write the guy a check right there. Seriously. Instead, I said as calmly as I could, "Really?"

"Yeah, it has some problems," he continued. "It hasn't been annexed into the city yet."

As nonchalantly as I could manage, I said, "Yep, that's a problem," but in my mind I was practically shouting, *We want this land!*

We drove back down to the church office, and I was trying not to reveal how excited I was. I said, "We'll need to think about it, and pray about it. . . ." I jotted down his phone number, we shook hands, and he left.

As soon as the man drove out of the parking lot, I went to one of my fellow associate pastors and said, "Let's go. I'm taking you up on the hill to look at a piece of property." We zipped across town and when we reached the parcel, I said, "We're buying this land."

My associate took one look around and said, "Oh, yeah! Um, how much?"

After discussing the property with the other leaders in the church, we put together an offer with twenty-two contingencies, including getting the land annexed into the city, and we worked through each step of the process. It took a lot of energy and God-given vision to get from where we started to where we ended up, but we didn't turn one spade of dirt until we had done a flyover of the property to map it then took that information to a civil engineer to develop a buildable site on twenty-two of the forty-nine acres. We got an estimate of what it would cost to prepare the site, then we brought our master planner in and said, "OK, if we had this plot, where would we site the buildings?"

Before we were done, we had to pioneer a road; move 277,000 cubic yards of dirt to balance, cut, and fill the property to make a level building site; and remove some gargantuan rocks. We bought the land for $2,500 per acre, and by the time we were ready to build we had paid $22,000 per buildable acre for the twenty-two acres we developed. In contrast to $50,000 per acre on the valley floor, we had ourselves a steal, especially when you factored in the visibility and the view.

We left some of the remaining acreage as raw land around the bottom edge of the property, but in the master plan we made provision eventually to bring in another road and parcel off some residential view lots, which we hoped to sell, thereby recouping some or all of our out-of-pocket expense for the land. That fringe of land sat undeveloped for more than a decade while the congregation focused on other priorities after I left the church, but in the past several years the church has begun selling those lots and still hopes to recover much of its original investment in the total property.

To put the size of this project into perspective, our congregation numbered just over a thousand at the beginning of the process. By the time we actually moved into the new building, we had grown to about fourteen hundred members. Before we closed escrow on the land, we had spent about $55,000 in design costs on what turned out to be a $2.3 million project.

The most significant factor in the site-selection process is prayer and staying open to what the Lord may be saying to you. God knows the time, He knows the particular piece of ground, He may be preparing the heart of the seller—who knows? The man who sold us our property had all sorts of plans to develop the land himself, but he finally got tired of tinkering with them and decided to sell the land instead.

Keys to Site Selection

The standard rule of thumb—location, location, location—holds true for church buildings as well as for homes and businesses, but other considerations are equally important. If you already own some land, is it adequate for your future needs? Are you landlocked, or is there room for future expansion? Do you need to relocate, or would moving undermine the focus of your mission? To fulfill your mission and vision, where is the optimum location for your ministry center? Is your location visible? Is it easily accessible? How do you get onto and off the property? Do traffic issues exist that need to be resolved before you can build? Will new issues arise as your congregation grows?

Your definition of an optimum location depends on how you've defined yourself as a church and what parameters are on your ministry. If you're in a neighborhood from which a lot of your members walk to church, your requirements are very different from those of a community church that must be located on a major thoroughfare or easily accessible from all parts of town.

A great location is a combination of proximity, visibility, accessibility, and suitability. Depending on what's available, you might have to relax your ideals when it comes to a specific site, but don't underestimate the importance and potential impact of your location. Wherever you decide to build your new facility, your congregation will be living with the consequences for years, even decades, to come.

One of the best site-selection decisions I've seen was made by a church in Orlando, Florida. A community-based congregation, they found property to build a five thousand-seat facility right at the intersection of two major commercial boulevards. The street on the third side is a major artery at the edge of a neighborhood, and the fourth side backs up to another parcel of land. The church bought another sizable lot diagonally across the street on the neighborhood side for overflow parking.

Access to the new building is outstanding—an important consideration for a regional church of that size, which draws its membership from all over the Orlando area. The property has two access points on each of the three contiguous roadways, a total of six driveways flowing into and out of the main parking lots directly onto major streets. Situated in the core of the city, and about a half mile off the interstate, it's a perfect location for that particular church.

Regardless of the size of your building, visibility and access are always important. Can newcomers find you? If they can see you from a major roadway, can they get to you? One of the most unfortunate site selections I've seen was made by a community-based church in the Southwest. Their building is visible from a major freeway but accessible only by means of a two-lane frontage road, which is routinely gridlocked by Sunday morning traffic. If the church leaders and their planners had thought more carefully about accessibility, they might have opted for a different location.

How Much Land Do We Need?

After location, the next important factor to consider is how much property you need. Based on your vision statement, your master plan, and your committee reports and requirements, you should be able to at least estimate how much land you will need. Site size often will dictate where you can locate because the prime core of your city may already be well developed. You might have to go out to a fringe area to get enough land to do what you intend to do.

To estimate the minimum amount of land you will need, multiply the number of sanctuary seats you intend to have by 200 square feet, then divide the result by 43,560 square feet in an acre. That's a very rough rule of thumb and is by no means overly generous in terms of space. Each specific site will require adjustments for topography, setbacks, building layout, and parking, but, generally speaking, two hundred square feet per seat will give you enough room for the sanctuary, halls, bathrooms, classrooms, anterooms, greenbelt, setbacks, and parking—all of the things the city is going to require.

Another rule of thumb for planning is to build your new sanctuary two to two-and-a-half times your current capacity, based on normal growth expectations. Anything less than that could start feeling cramped before long.

When to Start Looking for Land

If I pastored a church that didn't own a suitable piece of property, or if I knew that we were going to have to relocate, the first thing I would do, even while we were working on our vision statement and other preliminaries, would be to start looking at every reasonable lot in the area, to get a sense of what was available. I would pray with the other leaders, work with real estate people, and drive around town. If there was a high place in town, I'd go sit up there and pray over the city to open myself to the Lord's leading. It's never too early to keep an eye open for a strategic location, but it can easily become too late if you don't look ahead and try to anticipate your needs. Don't wait until your current facility is bursting at the seams before you start to plan, or you might be forced into an untenable situation in which you must alter your ministry substantially or move into temporary quarters.

Site selection can fall into any number of places on the timeline. Regardless of your overall schedule, if you have an opportunity to purchase a prime piece of real estate—one with sufficient size, great location, good access, and visibility—as long as you do all of your homework, you can pretty much buy it without much concern that it's going to be too small—unless you have an expansive vision that includes a five thousand-seat auditorium and a school.

If the right piece of land becomes available, even if you're ahead of the game as far as your planning process goes, it's probably OK to purchase it or at least to secure an option. At the very least, it would be worth getting your key leaders together to discuss it and make it a matter for prayer.

I know of a situation in a Western state in which some absolutely phenomenal land became available from the Bureau of Land Management (BLM). It was plenty big enough for what this particular church needed, and the location was superb. Even better, because the BLM was trying to unload this property, they were willing to sell it at a relatively low price and carry back financing on it for a period of time. Furthermore, the contract stipulated that if the property was built on by a certain date, the BLM would forgive part of the debt—and several other incentives were salted into the deal.

Given its prime location near the main business district of a sizable city, the property was probably worth $1.2 million. Instead, the church paid something like $500,000, which stretched them right to the limit, and maybe even a little beyond. In terms of their planning process, the timing was awful, but the opportunity was too good to pass up. Even if they would have eventually had to sell the land, they could have put a warehouse on it and recovered their investment—so there was zero risk from a loss-of-revenue perspective.

After careful and prayerful consideration, they bought the property and continued through their planning process. Today, the congregation is into the third phase of their building plan, and the church is growing and thriving, in part because of the strategic location of their facility. It doesn't happen that way all of the time, but this was one situation in which it made sense to jump in with both feet because the opportunity was just too good to pass up.

In another situation, a church wanted to move from its city location into the country to gain more room for future expansion. They bought some acreage but without considering the zoning laws and other issues. When the time came to build, they met with resistance from the surrounding landowners, who didn't want a church in that location. Eventually, after months of wrangling and trying to work things out, the church had to sell the property—and took a loss when the land sold for less than they had paid. Just because a property is available and appears suitable doesn't mean that it's the right choice for you. Do your homework.

When do you stretch to acquire a specific site? When a timely purchase is strategically in your best interest. But if purchasing the property would cut into essential ministry services, it's too big a stretch. At that point, you're impeding your mission—your reason for being—not enhancing it. Sometimes it's a tough call, which is why bathing the process in prayer is so important.

Chapter 9

AVOIDING PITS
AND PITFALLS

EVEN IF THE "PERFECT" lot becomes available, don't rush into a purchase without considering all the other elements—besides location, price, visibility, and access—that factor into a wise decision. When we acquired our church property in California, we wrote twenty-two contingencies into our offer, covering everything from zoning issues to soil quality to our need for a congregational vote to move ahead on securing the property. We knew that moving through the escrow process would take months and then years beyond that to actually build, and we didn't want to blunder into a decision just because the property "appeared" to be perfect.

Circumstances will vary from one situation to the next, but you always want to proceed with caution when evaluating the suitability of a specific piece of property. Don't be afraid to ask for contingencies to protect yourself from unknown factors that could render your land unbuildable. You don't want to find out after the fact that your ideal site is the former county dump or that the state is planning to annex your land for a freeway project. Potential pitfalls include government regulations, site-specific factors, and neighborhood issues.

Government Regulations

City and county zoning and other restrictions can adversely affect the suitability of a piece of property. Before you purchase land, regardless of whether it has been developed before, you will want to research thoroughly any municipal codes and requirements that might affect your plans.

- *Zoning.* Is your desired location zoned for building a church? If not, how easy are zoning changes in your municipality? What is the political temperature in your city for the type of facility you want to build? Is the community positively inclined toward churches?
- *Government planning issues.* Do any municipal master plan elements affect your site? If so, what are they? Does the city's master plan positively or negatively affect your property? These issues are often hidden unless you know which questions to ask. I know of a church that owns a piece of land where the state has a highway by-pass option that would go right through the middle of the property. Consequently, if the church tries to sell that property, there's a restriction on the title, placed there by the state that says that the land can be sold for only certain purposes. The highway by-pass option limits dramatically the marketability and value of the property. Do any city, county, or state rights of way or easements exist that would affect the property that you're considering for your building? Research these issues up front, before you get your heart set on a specific piece of land.
- *Municipal codes and restrictions.* What are the city's site requirements regarding setbacks, storm-water runoff, sidewalks, paving, and other issues? What kinds of restrictions pertain to occupancy of the building? For example, some municipalities will not issue an occupancy permit until all the landscaping is in. A lot of churches go in with the idea that they'll use volunteer help to

plant a few bushes and trees after the building is finished, only to find out that they cannot take occupancy until *everything* has been completed. They either have to put in the landscaping or put up a bond to cover the cost before they can get a use permit or a conditional occupancy permit. Municipal codes and restrictions can add expensive pieces to the overall design, and they must be factored into the budget.

- *Setback requirements.* The rules and standards established by your municipality will often alter or impede your plans for a given site. Your architect or planner should have this kind of information, but don't take anything for granted.
- *Parking restrictions.* Does your city base its parking space requirements on total square footage or on the size of the building footprint? How does the number of stories on your building affect the number of required parking spaces?
- *Permits.* Is a conditional use permit necessary? If so, what is required to obtain one?
- *Height restrictions.* I heard about a church in California that ran afoul of their city's height restriction ordinance. During the planning process, they had to send up helium weather balloons on all corners of the site at the height that the building would reach so that the data could be studied to ensure that their building wouldn't impede the view by any of the neighbors. Because of the community's height restrictions, the church encountered all kinds of hassles in getting approval for the structure they wanted to build. City ordinances and other restrictions are definitely things you should check before getting too far into your planning process, especially if you are planning a full-scale sanctuary, which might be a single-story building but will measure out at the same height as a two- or three-story building.

Ministering to Your Community

What is the political temperature of the city? Depending on how involved the members of your congregation have been in the political life of the city, the government officials might have a positive or a negative view of your church. If you intend to build a long-term ministry in your community, you really must become involved in the life of the community, including meeting your government and civic leaders, inviting them into the church, and exposing them to what's going on. I know a lot of pastors who put together what they call a "government day," for which they invite their local community leaders to the church on a Saturday for a program with a patriotic focus. Their purpose is to honor their leaders, pray specifically for them, and give them a sense of "connection" with the church. Community connections are very important, and you should build whatever bridges you can to facilitate the process.

Site-Specific Factors

Location and size are two very important elements in site selection, but other factors can also disrupt the process—and add thousands of dollars to your costs—if you don't pay attention.

- *Topography*. The lay of the land has a great deal to do with the cost of construction. If you have to excavate, fill, or put in a stem wall to bring your building up to grade, those tasks are all added expenses that usually aren't included in the initial architectural design.
- *Access to utilities*. Are public utilities readily accessible? The availability of water, sewer, electric, and natural gas services is obviously important and potentially expensive. Are the utilities *on* the site or just *to* the site? If they're not at least *to* the site, you're facing a major expense. I'm familiar with a church that bought a parcel of land and then found out that the closest utilities were a

quarter of a mile away. That little oversight added $250,000 to the cost of their project. Of course, it made it easier and less expensive for the next person who wanted to build on that street.

- *Traffic patterns.* Traffic flow in the area around the site is a very important consideration. It doesn't do you a whole lot of good if traffic is screaming past your site while people are trying to make a left-hand turn across a lane of traffic into or out of your driveway. Under certain circumstances the city might require that you install a left-hand turn lane and signal, which would add a hefty expense to your budget.
- *Expandability.* Look at the property surrounding your building site. Is there a chance to acquire at least a right of first refusal on some additional land so that you don't become landlocked?
- *Soils.* Do you have the right composition of soils to be able to build? Soil composition can be a major factor in determining the cost of construction because if you have to bring in tons of gravel or fill, or if you have to blast to get your foundation in, your costs will go up commensurably.

The Foolish Man Built His House upon the Sand

Soil composition is a major issue that, unfortunately, is often overlooked. If you're buying a parcel of land that is relatively flat, you might not give a lot of thought to what's under the surface. But don't forget that your foundation has to go into that ground, and if the soil is not of an appropriate composition to support that foundation, it can create a major expense. The classic horror story (and it's true!) is about a pastor, new in town, who saw a neat looking property that he felt was in a perfect area for the church. Without much consultation, he purchased the plot, only to find out later that he had bought the old city dump, which had been leveled and grassed over.

The church had to pay to have all of the old junk dug out before they could build—to the tune of a couple hundred thousand dollars. It pays to know the history of the land you propose to purchase.

Soil problems can range across the spectrum from excessive underground rock, which may require dynamite blasting to clear a footprint for the foundation, to insufficient compaction, to drainage issues or dozens of other possible complications. The issues will vary depending on your location—the soil in the Hawaiian Islands is different than the dirt in Omaha—but every area has its challenging soils. It isn't very expensive to run a soils test, so unless you know what's in the ground on which you want to build, it is vital to find out. I wouldn't buy any property without doing at least a minimal soils test, just to ensure that we could do what we wanted to do with our building project.

You must build the cost of excavation and site preparation into your overall real estate budget. Costs will vary based on the size, location, topography, and composition of your acreage. If you're wise, you will make soil composition one of the contingencies in your purchase agreement. In other words, you'll want to stipulate that the deal will not go through unless and until you have determined that the soil is suitable for what you want to build. Trust me on this: If you have to blast to run your sewer lines, it's not a good thing.

As important as a soil composition test is, it doesn't guarantee that you won't have problems. At the church I pastored in California, we did fourteen separate soil borings to test for composition because we knew that we were going to have to do a major excavation. The tests revealed nothing of significance, but the first time they ran a grader across the property, they pulled out a rock the size of a Volkswagen. We ended up having to blast in some areas because there was so much rock. In fact, when I left the pastorate to join Church Extension Plan, the congregation gave me a plaque that read, "Upon these rocks we have built our church."

A wise purchase agreement will take into consideration any issues that could come back to haunt you later, such as zoning, conditional use requirements, soils, or environmental issues (e.g., wetlands, buried oil tanks, or erosion control). If you're buying a city lot, for example, that either hasn't been built upon or of which you don't know the history, do a soils test and an environmental impact study to ensure that no contamination exists. If contamination is discovered, you won't be able to build until it's fixed, and cleanup can be very expensive. If any evidence turns up that a gas station or other source of possible contamination was on the property, ensure that the seller has the clean-up responsibility and not you. The seller is required to disclose the existence of a buried tank or other known hazards, but you, as the buyer, still must be diligent.

I know of a man in upstate New York who bought an old school building without even looking at the disclosure statements. When he applied for financing, the lender asked him, "Is asbestos in this school?"

"They've never had any fire problems in that school," the buyer replied. "Where would there be asbestos?"

The lender shook his head and said, "Have you ever heard of wrapped pipes or asbestos floor tiles?" It turned out that the place was loaded with asbestos, a real mess. In this case, the seller had disclosed the problem fully, but the buyer had failed to pay attention. You can never be too careful.

Neighborhood Issues

Whether you own an existing site or are planning to move, relations with the neighbors are a potential minefield. What is the attitude of the surrounding neighborhood toward the church? Is it positive? Negative? Ambivalent? Are your neighbors likely to support your building project or expansion, or will they try to throw roadblocks into your path? Have you been a good neighbor, or are there unresolved issues or conflicts just waiting to rear up?

Being a good neighbor begins even before you start to build—and maybe even before you purchase your property. Depending on the location of your site, it is usually a good idea to conduct at least an informal survey of the neighbors. Are they supportive of your building in their neighborhood? If only one or two neighbors are opposed, you can work to win them over and their opposition will probably not deter you. But if you have a neighborhood that is dead set against having a church in the area, it is probably wiser to excuse yourself graciously and go down the road, unless the site is absolutely golden and you're willing to work hard for acceptance. Based on the law of averages and some people's propensity for stirring up trouble, you'll always encounter *some* opposition, but an overwhelming backlash may well be the Lord's way of saying that He has a better location in mind.

If you have negative relationships in your neighborhood, you're better off resolving those issues as best you can before you launch into a building project. It's kind of like tilling the soil before you try to plant. You want to ensure that you've resolved any conflict. If a parking issue exists, if your neighbors are upset because people from the church are parking on the street, see what you can do right now to resolve the problem. Arrange with a nearby school or mall to allow parking there and shuttle people in. Do whatever it takes, but make your neighbors as happy as you possibly can because they will have a great deal of influence over whether your expansion plans will be successful.

Expanding in a Landlocked Neighborhood

Neighborhood relationships are even more important if your church is landlocked and the nearest available ground for building would take you beyond the area of your ministry. One solution is to try to buy up the houses or property around the church. Assuming that you've already established good relationships with your neighbors, I would recommend that any church that is landlocked but needs to expand should go to their neighbors and say, "I know you're not planning to move, but if you do decide to sell at some point, we would be delighted to work with you on a right of first refusal."

Your approach needn't be mercenary. Just simply and sincerely communicate with your neighbors that the church would be a willing participant in a purchase at fair market value, if and when they might choose to sell.

If some of your neighbors are elderly, you might talk to them about a charitable remainder trust, which is a tax-planning device that allows them to live in their house for free for as long as they need to, but then it provides for the title to revert to the church when the owner dies.

When you're landlocked, the very best thing you can do is be an excellent neighbor. Go above and beyond the call of duty to keep your neighbors happy. Ensure that your Sunday morning and midweek activities are not generating too much noise. Remind your congregation not to block driveways when parking and to drive courteously and carefully on neighborhood streets. If neighbors have concerns, ensure that they know who to call and that their complaint will receive prompt attention.

Make being a good neighbor a high-profile issue with your congregation. After you've laid the proper groundwork, you've almost earned the right to go to your nearest neighbors and say, "By the way, if downstream you determine that you want to sell, we would be very interested in talking with you." You might even enter into an immediate agreement for right of first refusal, but at least begin to establish the idea that you're interested in buying the property. First, of course, gain agreement from the city about zoning or conditional use. Don't start buying up the surrounding homes without ensuring that city ordinances will allow you to convert the properties for church use.

Buying up surrounding properties is a difficult process and not entirely desirable, but it is not all that uncommon. If all systems are go, ask a real estate agent to watch closely for neighboring properties to go on the market in case the owners don't talk to you first. Then, negotiate to buy the houses and start the process of determining an interim use. In the short term, you might try to rent the homes or use them as classrooms because you're not going to knock them down one at a time, and you might have one "holdout" property that you can't get. Don't be misled. Buying surrounding properties is an extremely complex, costly, and time-consuming approach, but if you're truly landlocked and your ministry vision would be compromised by a move, it might be your best option to work with what you have. The other possibility is to expand upward by adding a second story, but even then you might run into height restrictions, zoning requirements, revised parking requirements, or other obstacles thrown in by your neighbors or the city. The bottom line is this: the more background research and proactive preparation you do, the better your chances of avoiding the pits and pitfalls on the road to your new facility.

Chapter 10

SELECTING YOUR ARCHITECT

AFTER ALL OF THE preliminary steps have been completed, you should have enough information compiled to take to a master planner or architect. The more prepared you are and the more information you can provide, the smoother this part of the process will go and the better results you will achieve. Call other churches whose style of worship is similar to yours or whose buildings you admire and ask them who designed them. Interview several recommended architects. Be sensitive to how well each of the candidate's philosophies and programming processes intersect with your needs and desires. A "programming process" is the way in which the architect will translate your needs into projected space. It is essential that you understand the process that your architect will use because it will greatly influence your communication.

The complexity of your architect-selection procedure depends on the size of your project and whether it's a new building or simply a remodeling job. If you are remodeling, often it is easiest and most economical to go back to the architect who designed the original building because he will already have the plans.

If you're building from the ground up, any number of fine

commercial architects could do a great job of designing a church building, but if they have never built one, it is important during the interview stage to find out what resources they can draw upon to help them. Most architects won't try to design every phase themselves. They have staff support or colleagues with whom they work for specific types of space and for landscape design. If an architect says that he can do the whole thing himself, run for the nearest exit.

You might be well advised to enlist the services of one of the many architects across the country who specialize in churches. They might also design other types of buildings, but their primary focus is on churches. A church specialist is a good resource if you're building something of any significant size because designing church buildings presents some unique challenges. For example, an architect's acoustical qualifications really should be discussed as part of the selection process. Ask, "How do you handle the sound issues? Do you have that expertise on your staff or do you hire it in?"

When would you not choose a church specialist? If you had confidence in a local architect because you had seen his work, or because you had talked about the life of the church and he clearly understood your needs. Maybe he's never designed a church before, but if he has a passion to do it and his other credentials are sound, then you might want to take a chance and work with him. But there's really no substitute for experience.

Even when working with a specialist, it is important to explore the architect's own church background because his primary frame of reference will introduce certain blinders. If the only church the architect has ever attended meets in a rented warehouse or a converted shopping mall, his view of what a church looks like could affect your project. An architect from a liturgical church background will have an entirely different view of what the platform and altar area should look like than someone who grew up in a less formal worship setting. Different denominations assign different levels of prominence to the preaching of the Word, the celebration of the sacraments, and the ministry of the body. It is absolutely essential that your architect understand and appreciate your worship style and ministry priorities. If your style of worship includes frequent altar services, for example, you don't want an architect who will design a space that brings the front pew too close to the platform.

The simplest solution, perhaps, would be to hire an architect who has grown up in your type of fellowship or who has built a lot of churches for your style of worship. If he has experience building similar churches, chances are that he'll have a pretty good idea of what needs to be done in your case. Regardless of the architect's experience, however, I wouldn't hire him unless he had visited our church during a service to get a feel for how we worship—and I was confident that he understood our unique needs.

Keys for Selecting an Architect

Along with selecting your builder, choosing an architect will be the most important decision you make during the planning process. Unless your project is very small and very simple, you should interview more than one architect. This is no time to rush or take shortcuts. The more questions you ask, the more information you gather, and the more references you check, the more satisfied you will be with the results. If you're wise, you will evaluate thoroughly each architect's qualifications in the following four key areas:

1. skill and experience,
2. reputation,
3. chemistry, and
4. availability.

Skill and Experience

The best place to begin is by looking at finished projects. Pictures are nice, but you'll want to see as many buildings as you can in person. If possible, take your committee on a tour of several churches that the architects have designed. Do you like the way their buildings look?

Ask a lot of questions about the buildings they've done. What is their experience in working with contractors? How buildable are their plans? Are they easy to read and build?

Ask questions about their timelines and costs. With the resources they have, can they hit your deadlines? Are they willing to work to a budget as opposed to building the ultimate dream center? What is their track record for coming in on budget? How do they bill for their services? Is it based on a percentage of the total cost of the project (which is normal), or is it based on the budget? Most architects will have a boilerplate American Institute of Architects (AIA) contract, which has room to add your specifications.

How involved will they be in the ongoing process? What is their experience in working with church building committees? How do they handle reviewing the plans? How do they handle changes? What is their process for taking the plans through to a permit? Are they going to hand you a roll of plans and say, "OK, deliver these to the building department," or are they going to walk them through the process? Are they going to deal with the red lines and criticisms from the building department?

Will they supervise the project in the sense that they'll stop by for periodic spot checks to ensure that the contractor is building to plan? Usually, an architect will charge an additional fee for supervision. It might be 7 percent for drawing plans or 7.5 percent if he has supervision responsibilities.

Reputation

I cannot overemphasize the importance of checking references, yet far too many churches still fail to do it. You are really asking for trouble if you don't at least call the pastors of other churches the architect has designed. *Visiting* those churches would be even better, but you should at least talk to some pastors who have worked with the architect.

When you call the churches, it is *very* important to ask questions such as: How did the architect work with your building committee? Did you feel as though you had good communication? What was your experience with the architect's budget projections? Was he sensitive and responsive to your needs, limitations, and concerns? Were the plans readable and buildable for the contractor? How did the architect handle changes? Was he cooperative and helpful or was he resistant? Did you have any problems? Did the architect understand his appropriate role in the project?

Some architects develop a sense that it's their building. It's almost like pride of authorship for a writer. You would be wise to explore that angle with your references. "Did you have any situations where you wanted to add a door somewhere and the architect said, 'You're going to ruin my building'?" I have a straightforward answer for architects who take on too much "ownership" of a project. I simply say with a smile, "Hand over your checkbook and we'll do it your way."

Be sure to ask other pastors about building maintenance. "How well is your building designed for maintenance? Are there enough outlets so that you can vacuum all the way down the hall? Are the janitorial closets big enough and equipped properly (and are they where they need to be) so that you can maintain your building? Any leaks in the roof or windows? How is the HVAC (heating, ventilation, and air conditioning) coverage? Is there anything you would do differently if you had the chance?"

Ask a combination of specific and open-ended questions to elicit as much information as you can from previous customers of the architect. Again, the more information you can gather up front, the better your experience will be.

Depending on where your architect's other projects are, a phone conversation with his previous clients might be the best you can do. But you'll always be far better off if you can actually *go* to a church that the architect has built and walk around with somebody. If you can, walk with the janitor and the pastor, and ask all of your questions. Seeing is believing, and if you're in the building walking around, you might think of questions that would otherwise slip your mind. Also, if you walk through a local building that is really sharp, find out who the builder is and put his name at the top of your list of contractors to call.

Speaking of contractors, don't forget to talk with builders who have worked with the architect's plans, especially church plans. Ask two things: "Were the plans buildable?" and "How did the architect handle changes?" Sometimes an architect will draw some wonderful-looking plans, but when the contractor tries to build from those plans, corners don't match and roofing systems don't fit together. It's better to hear those stories in advance than to experience the reality for yourself.

Selecting References

If you ask a prospective architect for a list of references, he's going to give you a list of projects that went well. A more objective approach is to ask for a complete list of the projects he's built and then you select which ones to call. You're bound to get a more well rounded perspective that way.

Don't limit yourself to the architect's list of contacts. Another good source of information is the city planning office. What is the architect's reputation with the city planners and inspectors? If you find out that the staff at the building department dislikes a particular architect because he's difficult to work with, you might want to think long and hard before you hire him. The building department has the power to make your life miserable if they don't like your architect, your builder, your plans, or you. If they get along with your architect, though, he'll usually be able to maneuver things through the system for you.

Another important person to have on your side is the fire marshal. Does he approve of the placement of the sprinklers and how the exits are situated? When you have a building in which groups of people will be gathering, the fire marshal, if he wants, can make your life miserable.

Don't make the mistake of thinking that you can domineer or intimidate the civil servants who must sign off on your building. Come alongside them and express your willingness to comply with their standards and get along. The better you work together, the easier your project will go. Besides, every encounter during the building process is an opportunity for ministry. Don't lose sight of the big—eternal—picture.

Chemistry

Does the architect seem to understand your needs? Is he open to working with your specific needs, wants, and desires? Interpersonal chemistry is something to discuss with the members of your committee. It's an internal, in-house issue, not something you talk about in the interview. While you're listening to an architect's presentation, ask yourself, "Will I enjoy working with this guy? Or is he going to drive me nuts every time we have to meet?" If a candidate rubs you the wrong way, chances are the feelings are mutual. If the chemistry doesn't feel right, it probably isn't, and you probably shouldn't push it just because the architect happens to be local, cheap, or even good. Honest communication is so vital to the success of your project that you don't want to gloss over bad chemistry. It will come back to bite you—guaranteed.

Availability

Your search may uncover a great church designer, but if he's tied up with other projects during the time that you need him, you might want to look elsewhere.

How important is it that the architect or planner be local? It really isn't vital. Hiring someone from out of town does cost more because you have to pay their expenses to come in, but it's not vital to hire someone local. I would go with an out-of-town architect who was very well versed in church work over a local designer who wasn't. It depends on what kinds of resources are available in your community.

A local architect has the advantage in terms of communication and cost. It's almost always easier to communicate with someone who's local. You can visit his office, call him on the phone, or get together for lunch. It's a whole different thing with someone who flies in once a month. Both situations can work, but communicating with the out-of-town architect is more complicated. When you check references, ask other clients about their experience communicating with the architect.

Working with Your Architect

The architect is the core expert during the design and planning phase. Expertise, skill, foresight, and insight are the things for which you're paying. The planner is the one who is supposed to know what needs to be done and which experts need to be called into the process to move from the design phase through site development, building, and landscaping, to building occupancy and maintenance.

Ninety percent of the time, your architect will have connections with the necessary professionals, whether they are engineers (civil, soils, mechanical, and structural), interior designers, equipment suppliers, sources for fixtures (e.g., toilets, sinks, carpets, and pews) or acoustic professionals (very important). He might also have recommendations for building contractors and subcontractors, but don't let the designer's suggestions keep you from your own due diligence in selecting a builder.

The only time an architect's choices of other professionals become a significant issue is when you're building an especially large building or when you get feedback from other clients of the architect about certain problems. For example, if one of your references says, "The building's fine, but we have a little problem with heating and cooling," that's a red flag. To avoid the same problem, ask your planner, "What have you learned about HVAC since that project? Are you still using the same engineer and suppliers?"

Keep in mind that architects are in architectural "practice," just like a physician or a lawyer, and we are the people on whom they are practicing. Everyone learns as they go, so if a designer has a clinker in a particular area, you want to know what he's doing to avoid repeating that problem.

You might get an architect who says, "I don't want to work with a committee. I want to work with only one or two people." I don't blame him. If you have the architect work long-term with the whole committee, everybody will go nuts in the process—and your costs will go up. A more effective approach is to have an executive committee or an architect selection committee work directly with your planner. This committee can then make recommendations to the full committee. If you follow this path, you'll want to schedule a kind of "town-hall" meeting with the full committee and the architect before you get too far down the road to give everyone an opportunity to hear the architect's presentation and ask their questions. After the preliminary presentation, the ongoing interaction with the architect would be handled by the executive committee, which would meet with the designer regularly. The senior pastor, or somebody who represents him very well, should be a part of the executive committee so that the selection process doesn't get away from him. But, whatever you do, don't make the pastor the sole liaison with the architect. Spread the responsibility among three or four others to ensure that the communication remains full and rich and does not represent just one person's perspective. Having the full building committee draft a document for the executive committee to take to the architect can be very helpful.

Plan Review and Approval

What is the architect's process for working with the building committee through the preliminary plans? A good architect will take an active leadership role in working through the plans with the committee and soliciting comments, criticisms, feedback, and questions before he proceeds to the next phase. The architect should lay out the plans and walk the committee members through them page by page. Don't allow your planner to rush through this process.

A truly professional architect will walk his clients through every major decision, including any upscale elements he has designed into the plans or any options that will be more expensive. The architect's responsibility is to point out those issues and then let the clients make the call.

In your initial discussions with the architect, ensure that he understands that you want maximum bang for your buck but that he must keep the cost of the building within the budget. Walk him through your needs, wants, and desires, and make clear that you want him to work his way down the list, in order of priority, and meet the challenge of giving you all of your needs and as much as you can afford of your wants and desires.

Beware the architect who is tempted to build a monument to his own creativity to which he can point and say, "I built that, and it has maximum flexibility in the lighting system," to borrow an earlier example.

Communication is the key. Ask the right questions, and when you run out of questions, ask the architect, "What questions should I be asking that I'm not? What issues should I be concerned with that haven't surfaced yet?" The architect and the builder shouldn't laugh at or resent such questions unless they have their own agendas.

Chapter 11

DESIGNING YOUR SPACE

WHEN YOU SIT DOWN with your architect, be prepared to describe your church in living color. Now is the time to present the communication document that you and your building committee developed earlier (see chap. 6). At a bare minimum, your communication document should include a clear statement of the church's mission; vision; needs, wants, and dreams; and budget. But don't stop there. A well-written communication document will also explain the culture of your church, how you worship, how you interact with each other, and who you are as a congregation.

The more complete and comprehensive your communication with your architect, the better your chances of getting the building you need. Give him all of the demographics, including membership numbers, average weekly attendance, how many families are in the church (and how many kids), and how many people you expect to have at a series of checkpoints along the way. Walk the architect through the process of how you see the church growing over the next one, three, five, or ten years. Articulate the vision. Make clear where you're headed.

Answering All of the Architect's Questions

If I haven't made my point well enough by now, let me say it again: Your mission statement and your vision for your ministry will set the parameters for every other decision. Following are just a few of the many questions that will affect the specific elements of your space plan.

Are you a family church with programs for infants through senior citizens? Are you a seeker church, a neighborhood church, a revival center, a denominational church, or a community fellowship that draws people from all over the area? How does your philosophy of Christian education affect your building needs? Does your ministry include Sunday school, toddler care, maintenance ministries, counseling, Christian school, day care, adult education, seminars, or sports and recreation?

Do you need a separate chapel in addition to your main worship space? Do you need classrooms, break-out rooms, moveable walls, and flexible spaces? Counseling rooms with discreet entrances and exits? Fellowship halls and fireside rooms? A full gym with locker rooms and showers? Does the gym need to convert into fellowship space, or do you want (and can you afford) two separate facilities? Do you want carpet or hardwood floors? Are you planning to serve meals, just coffee, or nothing? Do you need on-site cooking facilities, or are your socials typically potluck oriented?

Where do you see your ministry developing in ways that might have ramifications for very specific structures? Are you planning to hire a sports pastor and start a community basketball league? Is drama or musical performance part of your worship or fellowship style? Do you need flexible use in your sanctuary, classrooms, or fellowship space?

If your vision anticipates rapid or extensive growth in numbers, ensure that your design allows for expansion, especially as it pertains to sanctuary seating, bathroom facilities, parking spaces, access requirements, classrooms, baby care, and traffic flow.

Such issues are factors that you will want to anticipate and deal with up front. The challenge for the designer is to devise a plan that is functional and aesthetically pleasing at each stage of expansion. You don't want your facility to look like a series of add-ons; you want it to look like it was professionally planned from the beginning.

Designing the Sanctuary

The main focal point in most church buildings is the sanctuary. Your congregation's worship style, aesthetic sensibilities, traditions, practical budgetary realities, and the overall needs of the ministry will all be factors in the design of this primary worship space.

The top three considerations in every sanctuary are as follows:

- comfort: enough leg room, adequate cushion and back support, moderate temperature and no drafts;
- sight lines: an unobstructed view of the platform and any projection screens; and
- sound and light: crisp, clear sound that is loud enough without being too loud and lighting that is bright enough to allow people to read the bulletin but that is easily dimmed for worship, drama presentations, overhead projection, and movies.

Other considerations include traffic flow—how you're going to move people in and out, especially with multiple worship services—and certain building code realities, such as minimum square feet per seat or occupant, required fire exits, etc. With code restrictions, compliance is essential.

Every space-planning decision ultimately ties back into the ministry of the church. Do you need a large platform for drama presentations? Do you need a baptistery as part of the structure, or do you go to a river or a swimming pool or use a baptismal font for your baptisms? Do you need room up front for altar calls? If so, how wide must the aisles be to accommodate people coming forward?

What about visibility? To preserve adequate sight lines, you cannot go more than thirteen rows deep without sloping the floor, elevating the platform, or building risers. As soon as you slope the floor or install risers, you eliminate many multipurpose uses for your auditorium. If you raise the platform, people in the front row will have to bend their necks to look up. Striking the proper balance between form and function is often a juggling act.

Sound quality is another very important consideration. Acoustics are affected by the shape and size of the room; the height, composition, and texture of the ceiling; the composition of the walls and floor; and the size and number of speakers, where they're placed, and how they're aimed. You need a designer who can evaluate all of these factors *before* the plan is built, someone who can determine accurately how the sound is going to travel, where the dead spots will be, and how to alleviate any problems. When the Crystal Cathedral first opened in Garden Grove, California, a person could not hear in some places in the sanctuary no matter how high the sound was turned up. The church had to retrofit the auditorium with support speakers to overcome that design glitch, which then necessitated the timing of delays so that the sound would reach all parts of the room at the same time.

An architect who builds a lot of churches or other auditoriums should have plenty of acoustical expertise, or know qualified professionals to whom he can subcontract. But don't take anything for granted. An otherwise qualified architect whose business is largely centered on office buildings or warehouses may have had acoustical training in college, but he may not have a practical sensitivity to the important issues for a church building.

If you want the architect to design a building that will reflect the priorities and personality of your congregation, you must be able to paint a vibrant picture of what your church is like. Invite your designer to come to some of your worship services to observe. He needs to see things in action. If he's going to design your sanctuary space, he must understand the worship style of the church.

I've been in some Assemblies of God churches that I know were designed by a Catholic. I can tell by the way the front of the sanctuary is set up—there's almost a chancel, and there's no room for holding an altar service. I've been in churches that have big choirs, but where no provision was made for a door directly off the platform. There's no way for the singers to get onto the platform except to come through the side door of the sanctuary and walk up the steps.

Is your church into drama? If you're doing dramatic presentations, you'll need room for backdrops, multidirectional entrances and exits, and a curtain to conceal the stage and the backstage area. Audio, video, multimedia, lights, acoustics, sight lines—all of these factors have far-reaching design implications.

The question is not "How do churches worship?" but "How does *our* church worship, and how do we *desire* to worship as we move into the future?" In some churches, if they have enough room on the platform for a song leader with a guitar or a keyboard, they're set. Other churches need room for a full orchestra—and if they don't have it, it's a disaster because their entire worship service is built around orchestral music. These considerations are not insignificant, and the architect needs to know what to allow for in the space plan. Of course, a well-conceived design will allow for flexibility because environmental factors will change and you might need to revise your approach just to keep your vision steady.

Color choices in the sanctuary are often a major battleground. You're better off enlisting an outside designer and responding to a list of recommendations than having the pastor's wife or an in-house committee do the design. Avoid faddish materials and colors. Think about the long-term impact of your decisions, both in building design and decoration.

The bottom line in all of these matters is communication. The more your architect knows and understands about your worship and ministry style and how you're planning to use your facility, the better equipped he will be to plan the space effectively and efficiently.

Designing Classroom Space

Some pastors are so focused on Sunday morning worship that they almost forget about the rest of the facility. The sanctuary is important, of course, but the architect needs to know just as much about how you function in your Sunday school classes. Are they discussion-style or classroom-style classes? Do the kids sit around tables or in rows of chairs? Do you have an adult Sunday school? How do the needs of the grown-ups differ from those of the kids? Do you need blackboards, marker boards, bulletin boards, or pull-down projection screens? Solid walls or movable partitions? Do you need break-out rooms? How much flexibility is required?

For example, if you want the capability to have a large adult class of one hundred to two hundred people but also need the ability to break the room down for several classes of fifteen to twenty people, you need partition walls. That's a major planning issue, with implications for structures and spans and how beams can be run.

Do you need multipurpose rooms to accommodate a private school during the week and a Sunday school on Sunday? What about your midweek gatherings? If you have a school on site, wear and tear becomes a major issue. All of these details are very important in the planning process, and the more information you can give your designer, the easier his job will be. Everything costs money, but undoing something always costs more than doing it right the first time.

Heating, ventilation, and air conditioning (HVAC) are important considerations in every part of the building, but it can be especially difficult to plan and modulate HVAC in your classroom areas, due to varying room sizes and heat loads, the need for flexibility, and the strategic placement of thermostats. Are you designing for the square footage of the room, the people load, or both? If you change the number of people in a room, it changes the heat load. If you have contiguous Sunday school rooms, how are you controlling or balancing the heating or cooling in each room? Where are your thermostats?

HVAC capacity might be mandated by your local building code such that you must install a certain number of tons for the total square footage, but it's important to project your needs as precisely as possible. If you create rooms to hold thirty people and design your HVAC accordingly, but then you never put more than fifteen people in a room, you will have overbought your HVAC at a cost of several thousand dollars per ton. That's why it is important to spend time at the vision-casting stage to get as firm a grip as possible on your downstream needs. As challenging as it is to make accurate projections, you don't want to underestimate or overestimate your needs. Dollar signs are attached to every decision, and some decisions are not easy to undo or modify. You don't want to be living with a bad decision for the next twenty-five years because you didn't take adequate time or attention to determine your vision correctly, clarify your needs, and communicate information clearly with your planner and your builder.

Designing Child-Care Space

A lot of families in our society are having their first child later in life, and parents are a lot more particular about the environment of the child-care facilities than we were thirty years ago when we were starting our family. Back then, most couples were happy just to have somebody who would care for the kids during the worship service. If the nursery was full of those old stacking cribs that looked like mini prison cells, no problem. Today, a young mother walking into one of those nurseries might say, "There's no way you're going to incarcerate my child."

She's looking for a bright, colorful, and warm-looking room with a trained staff and sterilized surfaces and toys—all of which are perfectly appropriate. It isn't that we didn't want those things thirty years ago, but our expectations were certainly different.

If you're going to reach families today, you must have adequate room and the proper facilities for keeping the place clean and sterile. If parents don't see a sink with some antiseptic soap, they get nervous. Likewise, if the room is cramped, old fashioned, or "not fun," they won't want to leave their kids there. All of these factors require serious long-range thinking and planning. You need to understand and anticipate the needs and expectations of your families.

Designing Administrative Space

Designing administrative space that will meet your changing needs is a matter of effective communication. Every architect will have some experience designing office space, but not every office space is appropriate for your specific needs. Your task is to depict accurately your level of activity and to communicate specifically how your office staff operates and how the space will be used. For example, does each pastor on your staff have an assistant or secretary? Does that person need to sit close to the pastor's office? If so, that could affect the space design. Do you use some sort of secretarial pool? Does everyone handle his or her own typing, letters, and phones? Does the church have its own printing or other duplicating equipment? If so, do you need a dedicated space for that? What about tape duplication or sound mixing?

Do you need flexible space in your administrative area? Do you prefer partitions and open areas or fixed office spaces? Remember, form follows function. Evaluate your current operations, anticipate your future growth needs, and design your space accordingly. Most churches end up with insufficient administrative space for their growth needs because at the outset nobody wants to build empty offices.

How much foot traffic goes through your offices each week? What other uses do you have for this space? For example, are you going to offer counseling services? If so, you'll want closed offices (or at least several private meeting rooms) and maybe even a separate entrance or exit for use by those people who are being counseled. You'll want the counseling rooms to be insulated for sound, so that people sitting outside can't hear what's going on inside.

Designing Fellowship Space

Depending on the size of your facility, you might have a separate fellowship space, or you might need a multiuse recreational and fellowship room, a combination sanctuary and fellowship hall, or a multipurpose space that serves as the sanctuary, fellowship hall, and private-school gymnasium. Is the space designed so that it can be made to look and feel like a gym on Monday night, a fellowship hall on Friday night, and a worship center on Sunday morning? Or does it always look like a gymnasium with a cross on the wall? And does it smell like a gymnasium?

Those are very challenging and subjective design situations, especially when you have fixed elements that can't be disguised—such as basketball backboards and scoreboards. Scheduling is always a challenge in multipurpose facilities, and one of the most important considerations in designing such spaces is how quickly and easily you can make the transition from one use to the next. Ensure that your architect understands exactly how the space will be used and what kind of flexibility must be designed into the room.

What other kinds of fellowship space are needed to fit your congregation's style? Do you need a fireside room for intimate gatherings, or just a big fellowship hall where you can host potlucks and serve banquets? Or do you need both? If you have a kitchen, does it need to be commercial grade or simply a household-style kitchen? Are you planning to prepare meals on-site, keep dishes warm for potlucks (with ample and well-placed outlets to plug in several crock pots), or will most of your events be supplied by a caterer? However you choose to use these facilities will be determined by your style of ministry and how much space you have available. Obviously, these decisions may have significant cost ramifications, building code implications, and specialized electrical, plumbing, and HVAC requirements. Whatever you decide, you must communicate effectively with your designer so that he can design the appropriate space for your needs.

How do you design a multipurpose facility with growth and expansion in mind? What is your long-term plan for a separate sanctuary? An experienced and qualified designer will be accustomed to situations where a church says, "Our current attendance is three hundred, but we're planning for significant growth. Initially, we want to build enough room for six hundred, but our vision is to grow to fifteen hundred." The designer might design a fan-shaped facility that can be expanded in stages. If you give the architect a clear vision of your long-range goals, he should be able to find a variety of ways to design flexibility into the original set of plans. Of course, tradeoffs are usually required to get what you want or need. You might have to compromise on your ultimate design to allow for expandability or flexibility. For example, you might have to design hallways such that they can be used for overflow seating or foyer space. If you're determined to have a sports outreach program but you can't afford a separate gym, you might have to put up with basketball standards on the side walls of the sanctuary—and a parquet floor instead of carpet—rather than building in the risers or sloped floor that you might prefer. Such decisions will force you to go back to your vision statement to ensure that your priorities and purposes are clear.

Designing Recreational and Outdoor Space

How much extra space do you have on your property? Can undeveloped areas be left "natural" or do you need to have a comprehensive landscaping plan in place before the city will issue an occupancy permit? Are your recreational activities primarily indoor or outdoor? Do you need a gym, and can you afford one? What kind of weather considerations, style considerations, space considerations, and topographical considerations come into play? How do traffic flow and building access affect your outdoor design? Do you need a drop-off and pick-up area? Do weather conditions ever make it uncomfortable to walk from the parking lot to the church? All of these factors affect how your outdoor and recreational spaces will be designed. Parking lots, landscaping, outdoor lighting, ball fields—everything costs money and creates aesthetic challenges for your designer.

A large-scale project likely will require the services of a professional space planner who might lay out a comprehensive long-term plan, complete with expandable parking lots, garden areas, water treatments, and lighted paths. It all depends on the size of your lot, the scope of your project, and the limitations of your budget.

Don't take your outdoor space for granted. Remember, the aesthetic appeal of your facility will be the first thing that neighbors and newcomers will see. And you get only one chance to make a good first impression. Also, don't assume that you can simply put a few shrubs in the ground and call it a landscaping plan. Check with the city to see what their requirements might be.

Designing Other Spaces

Maintenance is an often overlooked and unappreciated design consideration. It's amazing the number of churches that have floors that need to be mopped but no janitor's closet with a sink. Where is the water supposed to come from? The bathroom sink? Another common design oversight is a long, carpeted hallway with no outlets for the vacuum. Or two-story buildings with no janitor's closets upstairs. Dumb stuff. Obvious stuff. Sometimes it makes you wonder whether anybody thought about maintaining the building.

Church buildings are also notoriously short on storage space, especially if the church does drama and needs to store sets and costumes. Do you need secure storage for instruments or other valuables? Take stock of your storage needs and plan ahead.

Getting Outside Help

Don't be shy about enlisting the help of outside experts if it will help you plan a better facility. For example, if there is a thriving preschool in your community, you would be wise to ask the director to devote a few hours as an advisor to your committee on child-care issues. If you must pay for expert advice and the price is right, work it into the budget and do what you need to do to get that expertise into the mix. Hire outside advisors to the committee wherever you can afford them, wherever you sense the need, and wherever their expertise is not otherwise available. At the very least, it's absolutely essential that you find someone who understands construction issues if you don't already have that expertise on your committee.

You want to ensure that you have a well-qualified designer for each type of space you will need. Ask all of the questions you can think of, and then rely on your professionals to steer you right. A good architect will have staff or professional connections to give you a wide range of services. Ensure that the architect you select has the expertise and the horsepower to design the size and complexity of facility that you need.

Tips for Getting the Best Space Design

Identify your ministry style so that you will know what you want and need in your facility. Once you know what you're looking for, communicate, communicate, communicate with your designer. Ensure that you include in the planning process all of the key people who have a vested interest in each space within the building. Ask them to review and evaluate the plans to ensure that all of their needs, wants, and dreams have been addressed.

Regardless of which part of the facility you are designing, it is important that you communicate completely and clearly about how the church will function in that area. Communication between the building committee and the congregation and then back to the designer is absolutely critical. Effective communication is how you will ensure that you do not miss an important constituency within the church and how you can be certain to translate into the designer's mind all of the elements that must be considered.

When you review your plans, try to evaluate the layout of the building from the perspective of a first-time visitor. Is it obvious how to get from one place to another? Is the sanctuary easy to find? How about the classrooms? Are the bathrooms where you'd expect them to be? In some churches that I've visited, one entryway looks like any other and a newcomer would be afraid to open a door for fear he might end up on the platform—and be asked to preach the sermon! Look for the "invisible signs" that will make your building "user friendly."

Do you have a clear method of entry that makes it obvious which way to go? How inviting is your building to first-time visitors? Will they stumble around looking for help? Will they walk in and feel confused and lost, or will the building draw them in and make them feel at home? Ambiance is an important consideration, particularly when you're remodeling. You want to improve the user friendliness of your building—or at least not lose what you have.

We've emphasized the importance of asking your architect a lot of questions, but you should also encourage the architect to ask you and your committee members questions about your needs. Establish a dialogue in which questions and clarifications are going back and forth, and then carefully review the completed design based on what you told the architect that you needed. Don't assume anything. Space is not generic. It must be customized. And don't be afraid to make necessary changes—identified during the review process—to the plans. It's always less expensive to make adjustments early in the process, and it's better to make a change before the building is completed than to live with a bad design for the life of the facility.

The really hard work of preparing for a building project is defining your needs, wants, and desires and your styles and forms of worship because people get tired of talking about it. "How many times are we going to hash out the office space?" someone might ask. The answer is that you need to be willing to talk about it until you get it right, until you understand everything that you need and want in the space and can articulate that information to the people who are going to draw the plans. Remember, you're going to be living with the results for a very long time to come. There is no shortcut for the planning process.

Chapter 12

SELECTING YOUR BUILDER

ONCE YOUR ARCHITECT is on board and you have some plans from which to work, the next professional to hire is your building contractor. Based on your architect's estimates, you will have a ballpark idea of how much the construction should cost, but when you go out for bid with builders, you'll be nailing down the cost of the project to a relatively fixed number. It is beyond the scope of this book to discuss the nitty-gritty of construction bidding, but suffice it to say that, unless you are going to negotiate a bid with a particular contractor, you want to be sure to employ a fair and impartial bidding process. And, whatever you do, stay away from "cost-plus" or "time-and-materials" bids. A red flag should go up in your mind whenever a contractor is unwilling or unable to produce a firm bid. Cost-plus or time-and-materials bids leave a gaping hole for the contractor to pour in additional expenses, and they remove his incentive to control his costs and bring the project in on budget. Let the buyer beware.

The selection process for choosing a builder should be very similar to the steps by which you've selected your architect. Talk to several contractors, visit buildings they have built, and check their references thoroughly. How do you find professionals, contractors, and other suppliers whose values, work ethic, skills, vision, and expertise match or exceed the needs of the church? By prayer and due diligence. Ask the Lord for wisdom and discernment, and do a thorough job of researching and checking references. The primary factors you will want to explore are skill, experience, reputation, and chemistry.

Skill, Experience, and Reputation

There's no substitute for a good, qualified reference to help you select the right contractor. As with your architect, you want to ask your contractors to provide you with a complete list of their customers, and then choose for yourself which ones to call. Go out and visit completed projects. Talk to the owners and ask the tough questions. Does the builder leave his customers happy and satisfied with his work, or does he leave a trail of problems? Does he complete his projects on time and on budget? Are his buildings well built, or does he cut corners at the owner's expense? Do his buildings stand the test of time? Ask leading questions that encourage your contacts to expand on their answers and say what they really think.

We mentioned earlier the importance of your architect's maintaining a good working relationship with the city planning department. That principle goes double for your contractor. If the inspectors don't like the way he puts up a building or they don't think that he builds very well to code, they can throw a monkey wrench into your project by finding fault in every detail of the construction process. If, on the other hand, the inspectors know that your contractor builds good, solid buildings, he overbuilds and doesn't cut corners, the building department will be much easier to work with.

Keep in mind that your builder will be the primary contact between your church and the city building department. I wouldn't want anyone representing my church whose reputation was suspect. I don't mind if a guy is tough, but I don't want him to create problems that we don't need.

Key mistakes to avoid in selecting a builder include the following:

1. Don't pick a professional out of the Yellow Pages. The one you choose might be a great builder, but there's really no substitute for word-of-mouth recommendations from satisfied customers. Ask around and find out who the good builders are.
2. Don't take someone's recommendation without doing your own research and reference checking. Every building project is unique, and your needs might be entirely different from those of the person who gives you the recommendation. Referrals are a great starting point, but do your own homework to qualify a builder before you sign on the dotted line.
3. Don't shortcut the process. Ask the tough questions up front. Ask leading questions to identify any potential problem areas.

Chemistry

You'll be working closely with your contractor for nine or ten months during the construction process. Can you establish rapport and work with the one you select? Ten months can be an awfully long time if you get off on the wrong foot with your builder. You need to be able to trust him to give you the straight story about his progress and any proposed changes and to keep the project moving on time and on budget.

Beware of contractors who would lowball their bids with the hope of making back their profit margin on change orders. For example, a contractor might lower his profit margin on the overall building from 10 percent to 8 percent to get the job, but then he'll start writing change orders for every little thing and bill that work on a time-and-materials basis at a 20-percent margin. Some builders seem to think that if they can make enough changes during the building process, they will make back what they discounted up front. The best way to protect yourself from an unscrupulous contractor who plays the lowball/change-order game is to get a complete list of customers and then randomly call a number of them and ask specific questions. How did the process go? Did it seem that the contractor initiated a lot of change orders? Did the builder stick to his bid, or were a lot of modifications required to get the building the way the customer wanted it? The following section includes many more questions to ask when checking a builder's qualifications.

Qualifying Questions

First, does the contractor build on time? Can he manage a schedule? Is he able to get subcontractors in and out? Are all of the materials ready and the prep work done to keep the project moving? There's nothing worse from a scheduling standpoint than to have a subcontractor show up and either the materials aren't on hand or the previous process hasn't been completed. The problem is even worse if the subcontractors have brought along expensive equipment (especially if it is leased for the job) because everything costs money.

Second, does the contractor build on budget? How does he handle change orders? Avoid change orders whenever possible, and handle them as early in the design process as possible. Always ask for a firm bid on changes so that you can make your decision having counted the cost. If enough trust, experience, and relationship exists between you and the contractor that asking for a firm bid on every change might be deemed inappropriate, or if the scope of the job is small enough that bidding every change would waste time, then you might be safe to take your chances. But you should walk in with your eyes wide open. Every change-order decision hinges on its materiality and the size of the job, but unless you're talking about a fairly minor change, do not proceed on a time-and-materials or cost-plus basis. A firm bid (specified down to the wall plates) is more complicated and more time-consuming for your contractor to prepare, but it's the only way that you as the owner and keeper of the purse can really be protected.

Contractors often want to bill change orders on a time-and-materials basis. Don't fall into that trap. Always ask for a firm bid, and don't sign the change order until you have it. A typical conversation might go something like this:

> YOU: "I want to add a window that's not on the plan."
>
> BUILDER: "OK, we'll get to it next Monday. Here, just sign this change order."
>
> YOU: "No, I'd like for you to give me a price on it first."
>
> BUILDER: "Um . . . OK, but I'll have to get back to you."
>
> YOU: "That's fine. Let me know when you have a firm price."

Chances are, the contractor doesn't want to stop what he's doing to give you a price because it's going to cost him extra time today. Nevertheless, you want a price before you give the go-ahead. Only once have I said to a contractor, "Just build it," and it was only because he was a man I really trusted. I said, "I want to put a door in over there and turn that space into a closet." He didn't want to take the time right then to bid it out, but he said, "I'll tell you what. You trust me and I trust you. I'll put in the door and send you a bill for what it's worth. If you don't think it's worth what I charge, don't pay the invoice." He sent me a bill for $400, which was more than fair. The key is, you have to know your contractor, he has to have a high degree of credibility and integrity, and you must have supreme confidence in him. Know thyself and know thy contractor—and get a firm bid.

Third, ask your contractor—and definitely ask his references—how he responds to warranty claims. Does he warrant the building for a year? Does he show up to fix problems? Does he have someone dedicated to punch-list and warranty concerns, or does he have to pull someone off another job—and they'll get to it when they can? Obviously, if your roof is leaking in January, you want the contractor to give it prompt attention before it causes other problems.

Inevitably, every project will have some glitches—a door that doesn't latch or switchplates that don't match, for example. If it's a closet door that doesn't latch properly, it obviously isn't as crucial as an exterior door that doesn't latch. But even if the problem is "no big deal" (e.g., the wrong color switchplates were installed in the women's lounge), you want your contractor to take care of it in a timely fashion. Complications might be unavoidable in the building trades, but how your contractor handles these issues makes all the difference. His past customers will be able to give you the straight scoop on punch-list and warranty issues. Don't forget to ask.

Hiring Subcontractors

Most subcontractors will be hired by your general contractor, but it's a good idea to be aware of who is being hired in case you need to take steps to alleviate a problem or if you prefer one subcontractor over another (a member of your congregation, for example). If you do prefer a particular subcontractor, make sure that everyone is aware that you are specifying that person. If you're doing a negotiated bid, keep everything above board and out in the open.

When dealing with vendors or subcontractors, establish your terms right from the outset. Whether you're going out for open bid or working out a negotiated bid—whatever your process is going to be—make it very clear so that everyone knows the rules—and then stick by them. That way, everyone can feel good about the process and know that they were treated fairly.

Make clear from the outset that you are seeking a deal that is fair to all parties. Obviously, your desire is to build the building as economically as possible, but within that context you're seeking a fair deal for everyone.

To the extent that you've put together a good committee process, assembled a qualified team of advisors, and presented a professional image to your contractors or suppliers so they know that you're not just some overworked pastor who doesn't know the first thing about construction, you'll increase your chances of a smooth-running process.

Overseeing the Building Process

Hiring the right contractor is important, but keeping tabs on the building process is equally important. If you don't have the necessary expertise within your church to track the progress of the job, use your network and find someone. It's great if you have a qualified professional within your congregation who will volunteer to visit the site, review the plans, and ensure that everything is proceeding according to schedule, but if you have to hire an outside expert, do it. You'll be glad you did.

"I thought that's why we hired a building contractor, to oversee the construction process," one of your members might say. Granted, the builder's responsibility is to oversee the job, manage the schedule, hire the subcontractors; supply the necessary labor, expertise, and equipment to get the project done; and keep everything on track, but the builder also has a material interest in the job that might not always work in your favor. It never hurts to have someone watching out for your interests alone, someone who has no other ax to grind and who isn't employed by anyone else to do anything else on the job—especially if your project is big. Independent oversight is both prudent and practical.

It makes sense to acquire expertise when you realize that you don't have it within your congregation. One project that we financed—a church that was building a five thousand-seat sanctuary—not only had an architect and a contractor on the job but also hired their own engineer to oversee the project. It cost them an additional $60,000—against a $5 million budget—but the project engineer's sole responsibility was to ensure that everything was done on schedule and according to plan. He reviewed the plans and worked with the architect and contractor to keep things running smoothly so that when they said that they were 60 percent done, they were, in fact, 60 percent done. If the church had missed its budget in a particular area by a couple of percentage points, they would have spent more than the $60,000 it cost to hire the engineer, so on a project of that size, it made good sense to hire an expert full-time.

Even on much smaller projects, you would be wise to acquire an appropriate level of expertise to oversee your project. Be honest enough to admit that you don't know enough about construction to do the job yourself, and don't move forward until you plug the gap in your knowledge or expertise. Find someone who knows what's going on so that everyone can sleep well at night and your project will be done right, on time, and on budget.

Even in a small, eighty-member church, you ought to be able to find a contractor in the congregation, or in the network of the congregation, who is not tied into the project and can keep an eye on things. Or find a contractor in the community and say, "We'll pay you $200 a month to spend an hour or so on our site periodically to look things over and make sure it's all going right." Don't leave the success of your project to chance. Don't leave yourself exposed. Wisdom recognizes the advantage of using other people's knowledge at a reasonable cost.

It is the height of foolishness to think that you ought to be able to complete a full-scale construction project without your own expert—whose perspective isn't tempered by a profit motive—giving you a clear-eyed view of what's going on. Don't allow pride or insecurity to keep you from saying, "I don't know, but I'll find somebody who does."

Of course, you need to choose your experts carefully. I've seen some project managers who were certainly qualified but who had their own compulsive need for significance or their own ax to grind, which got in the way every time they felt they had to prove themselves or show off their expertise. That's not what you want.

Negotiating Bids

Enter every negotiation with Philippians 2:4 in mind: "Do not merely look out for your own personal interests, but also for the interests of others." Always be looking for win-win situations—which can sometimes be difficult to find in the building trades because most contractors are accustomed to getting hammered on and beaten down.

We have a responsibility to be good stewards, but we're also advised to give a man our cloak if he asks for our tunic. What's important is to keep things in balance. You cannot necessarily make an either-or statement. Certainly, we should not go to the mat over a disputed issue unless and until all other avenues of resolution or mediation have been exhausted. And, even then, we need to weigh out the importance of the particular issue against our desire to preserve our testimony before the watching world.

Balancing your Christian witness with the often hard-nosed realities of conducting business in a fallen world can create some delicate negotiating situations. And, as you know, working with other believers doesn't guarantee that there won't be conflict. In my years of lending to churches at CEP, we've had challenging moments when we've had to take a hard stand on certain issues. In situations where a church is perhaps trying to finance more than they can afford, and we've had to recommend that they scale back their project or we won't finance them, we've run up against people who have said, "We thought you were our brethren." Our answer is usually, "We are your brethren, but we're called to be partners, not fools. We need to be fair to all of the churches we serve. We're responsible to be good stewards of the resources that God has entrusted to us." Such moments are difficult because we always want to find a solution that leaves everyone with dignity, and where, as much as possible, everyone can win.

You will face times when, based on principle or a significant financial or liability exposure, you have a responsibility to protect the entity of the church and take a stand.

Competing Contractors within the Congregation

Depending on the size of your congregation, you might have several qualified contractors, subcontractors, or suppliers, all of whom want the bid, and all of whom are long-standing supporters of the church. How do you walk through this minefield without causing an explosion?

If I were the pastor in that situation, I would either meet with all of the potential bidders together or write them all a letter—or both—but I would go on record, saying to everyone, "We cherish each one of you as members of our congregation. We know that each of you has unique gifts and abilities, and we know that all of you are interested in bidding on this project. We're thankful for that, but we're also aware that not everyone can win the bid. We want to receive quotes from all of you, we want the entire process to be above board, and we want to be fair and evenhanded in our decision. Most of all, we hope that you have the grace and maturity to understand if your bid is not chosen."

If one of your resident contractors says, "Well, I was planning to *donate* twenty percent of the cost," you can say, "That's very generous of you, and as an individual you are free to do as the Lord leads, but the bid should be the bid."

The wise pastor and building committee will make all contracting decisions by open bid, keeping the process out in the open, and the final selection will be made by the committee as a whole, not by the pastor alone. For his own self-preservation, the pastor should be only one of many people involved in making the decision. In other words, he may be on the committee, but he should not be the deciding vote.

Also, if a member of the congregation intends to bid on the project, he shouldn't be on the building committee. At the very least, he should not be part of the decision-making process.

If someone in your congregation asks to do a negotiated bid, simply say, "Out of respect for you, let's not put you in a position where someone could criticize you or the church because they think we could have done the job better or more economically. We invite you to be one of the bidders, but we're going to go through an open bid process."

Are we saying that you should never do a negotiated bid? No, but recognize the pitfalls. Perhaps if you have a very high level of confidence in one individual or organization, and you just want to use them, you could show them your plans and negotiate a price. But the wisdom of that approach depends entirely on how much you know about what the project ought to cost and how much confidence you have in the contractor to give you the best deal. Negotiated bids are done all the time when sufficient confidence in a particular contractor exists, but a competitive process tends to bring out the best bids.

Regardless of which system you choose—whether an open or a negotiated bid—keep your selection process above reproach. Don't fall into the trap of soliciting bids from others just to get prices you can use to grind the contractor you've selected.

If you have advisors on your committee who are professionals in the same trades from which you're soliciting bids (but who have no financial interest in the project), even though they might be members of your congregation, their involvement in the decision making should be disclosed to all bidders. Even more importantly, any financial or material interest that members of your committee or your congregation have in the project must be disclosed and clarified so that everyone knows what's going on. Avoid conflicts of interest or leveraged situations.

When Titans Clash

How do you resolve a situation in which an "expert" in the congregation or on the committee disagrees with the "expert" you have hired either to advise you or to do part of the work? Follow the conflict-resolution principle outlined in Matthew 18:15–17 by sitting both parties down together in a room and saying, "You guys disagree. We love and respect you, Expert #1, as a member of our congregation, and we're paying you, Expert #2, to give us your professional advice or service. You two need to resolve this disagreement." Don't let a conflict simmer. If they can't work it out, then the pastor should sit in and facilitate the meeting. And if that doesn't work, you should bring in a third expert to mediate. Whatever you do, proceed in a controlled, biblical fashion. If you don't follow scriptural principles, if you respond in the flesh or by feelings, it will usually come back to bite you.

When you act as a facilitator, reinforce your respect and love for the parties involved, insist on not putting them into potentially compromising positions or situations that might lead to criticism or second-guessing down the road, and help those who disagree to work things out. Nip disagreements in the bud and follow the biblical pattern for resolving conflict.

Christian Versus Non-Christian Contractors

I've heard all of the arguments for and against using Christian or non-Christian contractors. When it all boils down, I would say to base your decision on the contractor's expertise and track record. If you're going in for heart surgery, you want the best surgeon money can buy. If he happens to be a Christian, great. The same goes for choosing a builder.

Never lose sight of the ultimate, long-term objective of winning souls for Christ. Don't fall into the trap of nickel-and-diming your contractors, trying to get the best deal, only to have them end up feeling as though the church was a skinflint client. I'm not saying that you roll over and let people take advantage of you, but I would rather turn the other cheek than ever have it be said that I took advantage of someone else. Model godly restraint, fairness, compassion, and patience in your dealings with everyone connected to the project. Remember, it's the Lord's project and the Lord's money, and He knows how best to use His resources.

Chapter 13

ADA AND OTHER CONSIDERATIONS

THE AMERICANS WITH Disabilities Act (ADA), which was written in part to ensure equal access to public facilities for people with disabilities, introduced building code requirements that will be part of any design equation. On a new building, your architect should ensure that all ADA requirements are satisfied as part of the original design, but you need to be careful if you are remodeling or adding on to your building. Remodeling even part of your facility could make you liable to comply with ADA standards throughout your entire building. ADA rules may require retrofitting or upgrading of existing facilities (such as rest rooms and entryways) even if they are not directly a part of your remodeling project. Even a minor remodeling job can result in expensive additional construction, such as building access ramps—or even installing an elevator. If you're already stretching your budget, ADA requirements can be a shocking and unwelcome surprise.

Who is responsible for ADA compliance? If you're using an architect, he will know what needs to be done. But if you're doing a relatively small job, perhaps using a contractor in the congregation, it will ultimately become the pastor's responsibility to ensure that the church complies. If you're not using an architect, you might want to convene a code-compliance subcommittee to research any relevant issues just to be safe. I always maintain that it's better to ask the questions up front than to find out later that you're not in compliance. Nobody wants to be surprised at final inspection.

Fire Code Considerations

A relatively minor alteration to your building can also have fire code implications. If you cross certain thresholds in terms of number of people in a room, or some other trip wire in the code, you might be required to install additional fire doors, provide extra exits, upgrade your sprinklers, or install an alarm system. Your remodeling plans might be modest, but the impact in terms of additional requirements can be huge.

I know of a church that did a remodeling job to close in an open-air mall outside the foyer. Because the weather was wet for much of the year in their part of the country, they couldn't use this area very often, so they decided to enclose it into a giant foyer and call it "the mall." Their design allowed them to segregate this area from the rest of the building, and they intended to use it for group meetings, social gatherings, and even small weddings.

During the design process, the fire marshal paid a visit. The church leaders already knew that they needed fire doors because it was such a big open space, but the fire marshal said that they also needed to add sprinklers throughout the building. Not just sprinklers in the new area, not just in the adjacent sanctuary, but in the entire building—all the way back to the new classrooms, the gym, everything, a total of 98,000 square feet. The church leaders swallowed hard and decided to proceed with the project, but it cost an *additional* $180,000, above and beyond the original budget.

Parking Considerations

Let's say that you want to increase the seating capacity of your sanctuary. You have some extra room in the foyer, so you decide to cut that space in half by moving a wall and adding two or three rows to the back of the sanctuary. Inside the building it's a fairly simple plan, but how will the additional seating affect your parking requirements? Does your community have an ordinance that says that you must have one parking space for every four seats? Do you have enough parking slots in your existing lot, or will you need to add some to accommodate the additional seating? Unless you already have excess parking (which is not likely at most churches), it might mean more paving, more striping, more money. Not having enough land for additional parking is where most churches get caught in the remodeling process.

Traffic flow is another significant concern. You could be in a municipality that says, "You're fine the way you are—until you grow. If you expand your building, you will need to add another driveway." Adding a driveway might mean purchasing an easement. You can see the dollar signs piling up.

I know of one facility for which the county said to the church leaders, "We'll grandfather everything in as is, but if you add *one more* parking space, you will need to install a turn signal out in the street." The county wants the turn signal *now*, because the church's traffic flow is such that they ought to have it, but they're not going to go back and make the church do it because they didn't require it at the outset. But if the church continues to grow, if they add one more parking space, they'll also be adding a turn signal and a turn lane—to the tune of about $250,000.

These types of issues present themselves when you start growing and remodeling. A lot of it is jurisdiction sensitive. If you're in a town that has a no-growth policy, those restrictions will dictate what you can do. If you're in a community that is especially concerned with traffic, or if you have neighbors who are upset and complaining, traffic control is going to be an issue. Some areas have noise limitations, height restrictions, or any number of other considerations.

I know of a Christian college that wanted to build a new

dormitory. Because of noise concerns expressed by neighbors whose homes were contiguous to the dorm site, the college decided to build the dorm with sealed windows and air-conditioning to prevent students from opening the windows while their boom boxes might be blaring. Having windows that don't open creates fire-code issues, of course, such as a need for wider hallways and additional exit points. Many building issues require similar trade-offs.

Evolving Community Standards

It isn't always an issue of safety or access for the disabled that causes problems in a remodeling job. Sometimes community standards change. One church set out to do a fairly modest expansion of their foyer to make more room for people to congregate between services and ended up having to pave their parking lot as a result. The church had been in the same location for years, and no one had ever complained about the parking lot, but the city had kind of "grown up" in the meantime and the community's standards had changed. As soon as the church filed for a permit to remodel the foyer, they hit a trip wire in the building code that forced them to pave the parking lot. Asphalt is very expensive and the difference in cost between gravel and pavement is astronomical. In this case, the additional requirement nearly doubled the cost of the church's project. If you decide to remodel even in an established building with a valid occupancy permit, hidden issues often can rear up and bite you. You must understand the standards and expectations of your community. You don't want surprises that end up doubling your costs.

Pulling Permits

You cannot take permits for granted because they may or may not be available because of cyclical environmental issues. Some areas of the nation have adopted a no-growth, hold-the-fort mentality that can transform the permitting process into a minefield. As soon as you apply for any kind of permit, you run up against all kinds of resistance.

When we were building in California, the big stink was over sewage capacity. Because of limitations at the processing plant, the county and the emerging municipality were using the sewer system to control growth. It became a real power struggle in that particular region. As a result, I became very involved in the community—as a private citizen—and I ended up serving on the subcommittee that wrote a new ordinance on acquiring sewer systems. When the ordinance was finally in place, our church was second in line behind a muffler shop that needed one additional bathroom. We needed fourteen toilets on our property, and we eventually got them. Fortunately, we had written "sewage issues" into our land purchase agreement, as one of the twenty-two contingencies, so the delays didn't come at our expense.

Code requirements will vary by region of the country and by municipality. In California, for example, earthquake safety is a major issue. In the Midwest or Southeast, it might be tornadoes or hurricanes. Often, the codes change over time as the government tries to cope with various natural disaster risks. If you have an older building, chances are that it's not built to the current code, and you might face expensive retrofitting requirements if you attempt even the simplest remodeling project. For example, you might be required to install foundation bolts or other devices to deal with earthquakes.

In some municipalities, you might have to apply for an additional permit if you change the use of your building in some way. Always check to see what kinds of ADA, fire code, and other building code requirements will affect your building before you get too far along with your project.

Insurance Considerations

If you're borrowing funds to complete your building project, your lender most likely will require "course of construction" insurance, which is not part of your regular coverage. If you have an existing building and are remodeling or adding on, you'll want to add a "course of construction" rider to cover the project. Your insurance carrier might ask your contractor to post a bond certifying that he has the necessary means to complete the project.

If you increase the size of your building, you might also increase the cost of your insurance because churches can be exposed to liability in so many different areas—elderly people descending stairs, a loose piece of carpet, spills, falls, trips—all kinds of stuff. Depending on the size of your facility, your insurance carrier might send a risk-management specialist to tour your facility for potential hazards. The underwriter might even offer some sort of discount if the church has an ongoing safety committee.

Following is an outline of a schedule of coverages that might be included in an insurance policy. Your insurance agent would, of course, tailor a specific program to your needs, but for purposes of illustration, the following coverages might be provided:

I. Property Insurance
   A. Property Covered
      1. Buildings you own (including permanently installed furniture, fixtures, equipment, glass, stained glass, organs, outdoor fixtures, and attached signs).
      2. Church personal property you own and personal property in your care, custody, or control.
      3. Building Ordinance Coverage—pays for losses resulting from enforcement of those building laws or ordinances that require that the property be rebuilt in accordance with current building codes. The three types of losses covered are
         a. Demolition Costs—the costs of demolition of the undamaged portion of a building.
         b. Value of Portion Demolished—the value of the

undamaged portion of the building that must be demolished.

c. Increased Cost of Construction—the increased cost to repair or rebuild the property caused by enforcement of building, zoning, or land-use law.

B. Covered Causes of Loss

"Risks" of direct physical loss or damage to covered property. This form will not cover certain designated perils, such as, but not limited to, nuclear hazards, war, smog, wear and tear, and flood.

C. Valuation Basis

Replacement cost, meaning the cost to repair or replace the property with like kind and quality without depreciation, unless the church elects not to build, in which case the loss is settled on an actual cash value (depreciated) basis.

D. Blanket Coverage Limit

Applies on a per-occurrence, per-location basis, with agreed amount endorsement provision—not to exceed replacement cost, or value shown on the statement of values on file with the insurance company, whichever is less.

E. Coverage Extensions Applicable. All amounts are per occurrence. "Included" means included in the blanket limit.

1. On-premises cleanup and removal of pollutants resulting from a covered loss (except asbestos)—$25,000

2. Fire Department service charges—$50,000

3. Buildings at newly acquired locations (limited to 180 days from date of acquisition) must be reported to the insurance company—$1,000,000

4. New construction at insured locations (limited to 180 days from date of acquisition) must be reported to the insurance company—$1,000,000

5. Church business personal property at newly acquired locations (limited to 180 days from date of acquisition) must be reported to the insurance company—$1,000,000

6. Miscellaneous unnamed locations coverage for small mobile equipment used on church premises, such as unlicensed motor scooters, ATVs, and other personal property (excluding trailers)—$100,000

7. Appurtenant structures—Included

8. Foundations—Included

9. Personal belongings owned by your employees, including the pastor, kept at the church for use by the church (in excess of personal insurance), per occurrence, per location (including theft)—$25,000 or more

10. Personal property of others at insured premises (in excess of personal insurance). Per person limit—$1,000; per occurrence, per location limit—$25,000

11. Property in your care, custody, and control—$100,000

12. Legal liability for damage to property leased or rented. Per location limit—$100,000 or more

13. Church-owned property off premises—Included

14. Church-owned property in transit, per shipment—$10,000 or more

15. Outdoor properties, including fences, radio/TV towers or satellite dishes, trees, shrubs, plants, and signs not attached to buildings (named peril basis, including wind peril)—Included

16. Mobile or modular homes (subject to same perils as buildings). No wind coverage provided within fifty miles of open water in the following states: Kansas, Oklahoma, Texas, Florida, Alabama, Mississippi, Georgia, Louisiana, North Carolina, and South Carolina—$50,000

17. Valuable papers—$25,000 or more
18. Demolition and increased cost of construction resulting from the enforcement of building laws and/or ordinances—up to a maximum of 25 percent of the amount paid for direct physical loss or damage, subject to maximum of $500,000 or more
19. Debris removal (if the loss is caused by a covered peril. This is a sub-limit and is part of the total scheduled limit.)—coverage is 25 percent of the amount paid for direct physical loss or damage, subject to maximum of $100,000
20. Glass coverage, including stained glass—Included
21. Backup of sewers, rising water—Included
22. Off-premises utility failure (including water, communications, and power supplies)—Included
23. Recharge of fire protection equipment—$25,000

F. Standard Deductible
1. $500 per occurrence, except:
   a. $1,000 per occurrence in the state of Texas (higher deductibles may apply in certain counties and parts of the South and East, as respects wind and/or hail).
   b. Different deductibles are shown on your quote as the above or on the individual Certificate of Participation.

   The deductible will be the responsibility of each insured entity. Churches are required to implement an effective loss-control program to assist in reduction of claims. High frequency losses will result in a higher deductible. Loss control employees are available to assist.

II. Boiler and Machinery Coverage—Equipment Breakdown Coverage

A. Heating, ventilating, air conditioning, computer equipment
B. Refrigeration equipment. Covers explosion and spoilage

Chapter 14

HAPPILY EVER AFTER: MAINTENANCE

AN OFTEN OVERLOOKED BUT absolutely essential element of the design process is planning for maintenance. Once you have your beautiful new building completed, how are you going to keep it clean? Where will all of the maintenance facilities be located? Has your designer included a sufficient number of janitorial closets with mop sinks and enough room for all of the necessary equipment? Are enough power outlets installed along the hallways to accommodate vacuuming?

These are the kinds of questions that you should ask your architect up front. Ask early because if he overlooks something important, like a janitor's closet for example, it is very difficult to fix later. How can you install a mop sink in the middle of a hallway if there's no closet? First, you have to create the space and bring in the plumbing. Take care of these details in the planning process to avoid expensive and disruptive changes later.

Based on the number and placement of your bathrooms, where will you store supplies close at hand? And do you have a plan for keeping the bathrooms clean and fresh? Is adequate storage provided for janitorial supplies and equipment? They won't fit in just any closet. You need to allow space.

Within the constraints of your design, you want to ensure that your surfaces are washable because you'll have continuous traffic as people come and go. You don't want paint that you can't wash or at least wipe down.

Planning for Upkeep

As part of the design process, your building committee should establish a maintenance schedule. Your master planner may give you some general guidelines, but you need to develop a specific plan to follow the manufacturer's maintenance recommendations. For example, when should the building be painted both inside and outside? How and when should the roof be maintained? What kind of treatment does it need? How often should furnace filters be replaced, and what other HVAC maintenance is necessary? I know of a church that was ready to sue their contractor because of problems with the HVAC. When the service technician came out to evaluate the situation, he discovered that the heating system filters had never been changed, and they were clogged with dirt and debris. No wonder the compressor blew.

How about replacing fluorescent lighting tubes? That seems like a simple task until you're standing on the sanctuary floor gazing up at light fixtures twenty feet above your head. You can't just climb up and stand on a ladder; you need the right kind of equipment. In some sanctuaries, you would need a scaffolding system to reach the lights safely, not just because that's the right way do it but also because of the legal liability and Occupational Safety and Health Administration issues that might stem from not doing the job correctly.

If you have a difficult maintenance situation—such as a chandelier that hangs twenty feet above the floor—work out with your designer how maintenance will be handled. How will you dust it, clean it, and change the bulbs? You might need to buy light bulbs based on their estimated life and then follow a replacement routine to change all of the bulbs at the same time before a critical number burn out. You're not going to want to climb up there every time a single bulb burns out.

Carpet maintenance: Any carpet manufacturer will tell you that a carpet will wear faster if it gets grit and dirt down into the pile than if you keep it clean. Regular vacuuming and periodic shampooing not only keep the carpets looking nice, but they also extend its life. It's much less expensive to maintain a rug than to replace it, especially if there is a lot of labor involved in undoing pews and moving them out and then bolting them back down again. High-traffic areas require a high-traffic maintenance plan to keep the floors and walls clean and the fixtures functioning.

Outside maintenance: Having a weed patch out front, or a dead lawn, or beer cans scattered across the parking lot doesn't look good. How are you going to maintain the landscaping, parking lots, and building exteriors? A lot of churches do it with volunteer labor, either weekend gardeners or retired or semiretired folks who like to keep busy. If your congregation has people with such gifts and interests, and if your volunteers are willing to do the work regularly, that's great. But don't leave outside maintenance to chance. Develop a plan.

In some communities, maintenance includes dealing with graffiti. The best solution for graffiti and vandalism is to have a can of paint on hand so that it can be painted over immediately. No matter how many times they come back or how many times you have to paint over it, do it immediately. Sooner or later, the taggers will get tired of messing with you; meanwhile, your building will look the best it can.

What's most important is that the grounds surrounding your building look sharp on Sunday morning because the outside environment is the first thing that people will see. For the sake of your neighbors, it should look sharp the other six days of the week as well. If the outside facility isn't sharp, it doesn't speak well for what's going on inside. "If they can't mow the lawn and keep the weeds down, how much attention does the pastor give to preparing his sermons?"

Planning for Depreciation

Everything in a building has an expected life, but chances are that if you're focused on your ministry and expanding according to plan, you're going to be doing some sort of project—either remodeling, adding on, or building—every five to seven years. Issues of obsolescence and life span should be taken care of as a matter of course in that process.

By contrast, you should plan for a very short window on the technology side (e.g., PowerPoint, projectors, and multimedia) before you'll want or need to replace or upgrade your equipment. When the time comes, your equipment may still be perfectly suitable for its purpose and you may choose not to replace it, but you'll want to plan for upgrading according to an estimated schedule of obsolescence so that the money will be available in your budget.

Maintenance as Stewardship

A lot of pastors and parishioners don't like to talk about the ministry of the church as a "product," but the fact of the matter is that people form opinions based on appearances. If your facility looks dumpy, visitors won't come back. They'll go to the place down the street that looks crisp and clean. Our society has high expectations. Your facility must reflect the standards of the community you are trying to reach—not too little and not too much.

If you can't afford to go top of the line, do the very best you can with what you can afford. If you truly have a vision for reaching your community, you must present an appearance that is attractive to the people in your community. The church should model the same excellence that God models in His creation. We invest in high-quality facilities so that we can reach people. We're not going for top of the line just for its own sake; we are investing in the future and in people's lives, and we must spend what is necessary to fit our niche.

If you want to live happily ever after in your building, it pays to recognize that your stewardship responsibilities extend to your building and grounds. If you view your facility as a piece of ministry equipment, an outreach tool to help you reach your community, how are you going to maintain it so that it looks sharp and is clean, pleasant, and inviting? Maintenance is basic stuff, but if you don't have a schedule and a plan, it tends to get overlooked.

If you want your building to be an asset to your ministry rather than a hindrance or an embarrassment, maintenance is crucial. If people walk in on Sunday morning and see debris on the floor in the foyer because it wasn't vacuumed, that sends a subliminal message about the quality of everything else in the church. It's like putting the tray table down on an airplane and finding coffee stains on it. I don't know about you, but the first thing that goes through my mind is, "Hmm, if they don't wipe down the tray tables, I wonder how well they service the engines?" If you don't take care of the little things, how can others be certain that the important stuff is getting the proper attention?

Your building should be viewed not as a necessary evil and not as merely a capital investment but as a place to house ministry, a tool for outreach—and it ought to be inviting. Maintenance has everything to do with how inviting your facility will be.

Regular upkeep also preserves your building's cost-effectiveness. If you are forever playing catch-up with deferred maintenance issues, you'll spend a lot of additional money in the process. It is far better to deal with maintenance issues as you go.

If you've invested a significant amount of money in your building, you have both a stewardship and an ethical responsibility—as well as a practical incentive—to expend both the money and the effort to maintain it. Otherwise, it depreciates and deteriorates right before your eyes.

Even if your congregation is small and you can't afford a full-time custodian, even if you rely on volunteers, you still need a maintenance schedule. In fact, a schedule is even more important if you are relying on volunteers because you need some accountability to ensure that the maintenance activities happen often enough and well enough to keep the building in good shape. Develop a checklist of things to be done, and appoint someone to follow up regularly to ensure that the facility is in top condition. It's great to use volunteers wherever possible to keep costs down, but you still have to ensure that the quality is maintained and the work is done.

You can have wonderful, well-meaning people who want to do the right thing, but if they aren't skilled or experienced, you need to train them to a level of competence that meets the need, or you need some sort of supervision that models the right way and ensures that the job is being done properly.

Maintenance Begins at the Top

When you walk down the hall in your church and see a piece of paper on the ground, do you stop to pick it up, or do you walk on by? I'm not saying that the pastor should wear the janitor's hat and do all of the cleaning and maintenance. It doesn't do any good for the preacher to be in the bathroom with a plunger when he's supposed to be in the pulpit or preparing his sermon, but neither does it serve the body if he ignores obvious problems that need to be fixed. Leadership has a lot to do with setting the right example and establishing priorities. A pastor should do everything he can appropriately do himself and find someone else who can and will do the rest.

The point is that maintenance is not a minimal or casual issue. It's not an afterthought, a necessary evil, or something merely to tolerate. It is a key element to keeping the building fresh and making it appealing for your congregation and visitors. Regular maintenance respects those who are giving regularly to the church. After all, they are putting their tithes and offerings into the storehouse, and they ought to be able to see that their investment is being treated with respect.

If you are launching out on a new building project or remodeling your existing facility, this is where the adventure begins. My prayer is that God will grant you vision and direction and that this book will provide a road map for you to follow. Blessings!